Praise for *The Creative Outlet Method*

"*The Creative Outlet Method* is an amazing assortment of activities to make group participation (and skill-building!) fun and exciting for all children, including those who need structure and guidance to successfully interact with friends and peers. Step-by-step instructions, lists of needed items, and supplemental materials are included, making it super-easy for families and caregivers to create successful performances at home or anywhere!"

—**Kathy Brill**, M.Ed., M.P.S.,
Co-Founder of Parent to Parent USA,
disability advocate, and consultant

"Developing the creativity of children with disabilities is often overlooked when focused on other essential life skills. Joshua recognizes the benefits of living a creative life, and his book provides a comprehensive, user-friendly guide for families and professionals to nurture children's creativity while simultaneously growing their communication, social skills, positive behavior, and joy."

—**Kristina R. Berzina**,
veteran special education teacher

"Parents, teachers, therapists, and caregivers will be thrilled to add these unique, theatrical activities to their toolbox for engaging with children. Joshua's method is a collaborative, fun way for kids to build skills, and utilizes a strengths-based approach. This method not only applies to special needs and neurodiverse children and adolescents, but it can also be used with neurotypical and combined groups!"

—**Sarah B. Silverman**, PsyD,
licensed psychologist

"Joshua Levy has woven aspects of explicit instruction, applied behavior analysis, and social skills training into a book that parents, teachers, and anyone who works with children with special needs can use proactively to improve interactions and positive outcomes. His experiences and passion for storytelling and theater provide a unique gestalt for learning. The activities in this book include many parts yet the totality of experiences and benefits goes beyond their individual combinations."

—**Dr. John W. Maag**, Larry & Sharon Roos
Professor of Special Education at the
University of Nebraska–Lincoln,
author of *Parenting Without Punishment*,
a Parents' Choice Award recipient

BY JOSHUA LEVY, MEd, MBA

THE CREATIVE OUTLET METHOD

At-Home Activities for Children with Special Needs

With a Foreword by Elizabeth Hampton, MA, CCC-SL, Associate Director, The University of Texas at Austin Michael and Tami Lang Stuttering Institute

Austin, TX 2022

JB JOSSEY-BASS™
A Wiley Brand

Published by Jossey-Bass A Wiley Brand
111 River St
Hoboken, New Jersey 07030
www.josseybass.com

Jossey-Bass books and products are available through most bookstores. To contact Jossey-Bass directly call our Customer Care Department within the U.S. at 800-956-7739, outside the U.S. at 317-572-3986, or fax 317-572-4002.

Wiley publishes in a variety of print and electronic formats and by print-on-demand. Some material included with standard print versions of this book may not be included in e-books or in print-on-demand. If this book refers to media such as a CD or DVD that is not included in the version you purchased, you may download this material at http://booksupport.wiley.com. For more information about Wiley products, visit www.wiley.com.

Library of Congress Cataloging-in-Publication Data is Available:

ISBN 9781119873495 (Paperback)
ISBN 9781119873501 (ePDF)
ISBN 9781119873518 (ePub)

Cover Design: Paul McCarthy
Cover Art: © Getty Images: (Children on Stage): Adam Taylor
(Wheelchair): Design Pics/Ron Nickel

SKY10035508_072822

This book is dedicated to—

Mom and Dad for believing in me well beyond "The Spaceship of the Rain."

My sister Jenny for all that Shazz.

My wife, Lori, daughter, Shayna, and son, Noah, for putting up with the world's best Dad jokes of all time, around the clock.

Contents

Foreword

Like most families, between soccer games, dance classes, birthday parties, and keeping up with the household, Saturdays in our house are jam-packed. Therefore I know my meeting with Joshua Levy was meant to be. The universe had to be in perfect alignment for us to be available and seeking out an activity on a Saturday morning. This is how my husband and I found ourselves with our (then) six-year-old-daughter at the Barrel O' Fun event space, taking part in a Joshua's Stage improv class led by Joshua. As I observed him at work, engaging the children of all ages in puppet making, improv, and role play, I was struck by his enthusiasm, his connection with the children, and the clear intentions of each activity that he presented to his active, participatory, young audience. As a practicing speech-language pathologist, it was apparent to me that while he ensured the children were having fun, he was simultaneously helping them grow their confidence as communicators, *and* he was also modeling how parents and caregivers could provide the same opportunities at home.

This is the heart of Joshua Levy's *The Creative Outlet Method: At-Home Activities for Children with Special Needs*. Joshua recognizes that all children want to participate and communicate, but what that looks like for each one is different. In this practical, how-to guide, Joshua has provided encouraging techniques and meaningful activities to spark fun and performance and that meet a range of learning styles, allowing for each child to feel welcome, heard, encouraged, and successful. The approach provides parents, teachers, and caregivers with clear instructions for how to lead children to grow their creative expression, and to further develop their self-confidence and their self-esteem.

What grew from my first meeting with Joshua Levy was an opportunity for the two of us to collaborate as he has lent his Creative Outlet Method to support the goals of the Michael and Tami Lang Stuttering Institute at the University of Texas at Austin's Targeting Communication Excellence programming for children who stutter. I have witnessed the joy his work has brought to both our participants and their parents as they have taken part in the Eye Contact Clap and the Ferris Wheel Round of Applause, turned into magical rocks, made pizza before our eyes (no food required!), and performed the most elaborate of stories, all within an hour's time. This is a group of children who all communicate in different ways: Some are outgoing, some are shy, some stutter, some are siblings who have come along for the ride, but all of them are having fun while communicating and interacting in new and innovative ways.

It is Joshua Levy's unique background as a special educator, educational administrator, and consultant that has given him the talent to develop the Creative Outlet Method and book that supports the creative expression of all children. In addition, his fun-loving personality, empathy, and positivity contribute to his foundational belief that all children should have the opportunity to perform and share their talents in an affirming and successful way. His book provides parents, caregivers, and educators the tools they need to do just that. Have fun as you share and implement these activities with the children you love to bring them much joy and creative growth.

Elizabeth Hampton,
MA, CCC-SLP

Acknowledgments

I discovered my creative spirit at an early age, and it continues to shine with me to this day. My upbringing, experiences, and background led me to founding Joshua's Stage, and from that endeavor I developed *The Creative Outlet Method*. I am sincerely humbled by the people who profoundly influenced me as both an author and educational entrepreneur, and who continue to impact my personal growth.

Since my immediate family has embraced my vegan cooking, it is only fair that I start with them. I am most appreciative of my beautiful wife, Lori, our amazing children, Shayna and Noah, and our three dogs (who also tend to enjoy my cooking) – Husker, Sophie, and Zoey – for supporting me while I wrote this book. Mom and Dad, for encouraging me to just be JBL, and for wisely advising me to always be nice to everyone because I never know when I will see them again. My sister, Jenny, for being a wonderful creative partner through our endless adventures in songwriting, silly dances, and full-scale dramatic productions, and for being my friend. My aunts, uncles, cousins, grandparents, and in-laws for supporting my creativity.

Kristina Berzina, my friend who gets my out-of-the-box thinking and for reviewing this book.

Shelley Anne Friend, I am blessed by your inspiration, guidance, and love for our family. Thank you, Naomi Ritchie, for your support and love for our family – I loved how John made everyone feel like the most important person in the world. To Gregg and Michelle Philipson for your friendship and for loving our family.

Kristi Boeckmann, for introducing me to the world of teaching special education at Eisenhower Middle School in San Antonio, Texas. Saralee Robbins, for guiding me as a teaching assistant for a Sunday School special needs class at Temple Israel in Westport, Connecticut. The Mary Cariola Center in Rochester, New York, for allowing me the opportunity to work with children with significant cognitive and physical disabilities. Kim Rosenthal, for supervising my special education student teaching experiences at Humann Elementary in Lincoln, Nebraska.

Dr. John Traphagan, my friend and mentor, for initially leading the Joshua's Stage cause.

Alicia Garnes, for supporting and fine-tuning the words to the Joshua's Stage vision during soccer practices and coffee. Todd Wilson, for continuing to lead and inspire the cause for Joshua's Stage. Bob Shaver of SCORE–Austin, thank you for your mentorship and valuable insight.

Matthew Brutsche, who taught me to think of something exclusive. Adia Dawn, for helping me map out the *Creative Outlet Method*.

Thank you to the families who sign up for programs with Joshua's Stage, especially the Ankeney, Eppes, Yaeger, and Lees families.

Thank you to the organizations who invite Joshua's Stage to conduct workshops with your participants. Thank you, Elizabeth Hampton, associate director of the Michael and Tami Lang Stuttering Institute at the University of Texas at Austin, for inviting Joshua's Stage to your organization, and for writing the foreword to this book. To Adrienne Barnett and Rachel Hamilton at the Thinkery, for supporting Joshua's Stage and my endeavors. Much appreciation for Chad Dike at the ZACH Theatre and Kristin Henn at the Move Your Tale and Excused Absence improv programs for collaborating with Joshua's Stage. Thank you, Maria Hernandez with VELA, for promoting Joshua's Stage to your organization's families. Thanks, Coach Jason Williams of The Fitness School, for supporting Joshua's Stage, and for your motivational pep talks when I needed them the most.

Thank you to the staff and families at the Capitol School of Austin and at William's Community School for embracing the Joshua's Stage after-school program. My sincerest gratitude to Jeannette Young, Kara Huss, and Suzanne Byrne for your support, encouragement, and guidance.

To the Temple Beth Shalom community, for opening your hearts to Joshua's Stage, especially to Rabbi Amy Cohen,

Jordan Magidson, Jeremy Moran, and Alice Marsel.

Instructors and volunteers at Joshua's Stage who foster *The Creative Outlet Method*: shout-outs to Josh Kuehner, Brooke Conway, Maggie Moore, Anna Westbrook, Luke Wallens, Laura Nagy, Sara Shapiro, Jen Mattson, Pam McDonald, Amanda Varcelotti, Tatum English, Mel Cole, Joy Goldfin, JoLynn Riojas, Daniel Brantley, Amber Kirk, Sam McDonald, Catherine Conner, Sarah Carder, Kim Dragon, and Jackson Sutton.

Thank you, Dr. Jon Pierce, for inviting me to teach adults with disabilities at the University of Texas.

Special thanks to the Weiner, Septimus, and Fricke families for carpools and for looking after the kids while I was building Joshua's Stage.

Thank you to the Greenleaf publishing team for copy editing and proofreading the manuscript. Thank you, Morris Publishing, for printing my self-published version of this book. Thank you, Jossey-Bass/Wiley Publishing, for bringing this book to even greater heights.

Preface

Throughout my nine-year career as a special education teacher and assistant principal, I experienced children with special needs demonstrating aggressive and challenging behaviors including hitting, punching, damaging property, using profanity, leaving school grounds, and screaming excessively. While many of the children had a Behavior Intervention Plan included in their Individual Education Plan, the consequences for their actions seemed to outweigh the positive rewards for their better behaviors. While I instituted token economy systems in my classrooms, I felt that I did not have a firm grasp on catching kids being good. I continuously wore the feelings of wanting to do more for my students like wearing an old shirt every day.

When I was seven years old, I started writing stories and plays, beginning with "The Spaceship of the Rain," my story of a boy and girl being visited by an alien, only to be killed by the alien – which my parents nevertheless applauded. I was motivated to further lean into my creative spirit. I proudly produced, directed, and performed an original play, "Jackie the Realtor," in my bedroom, where my sister Jenny starred as Jackie.

My core values are compassion, empathy, and sincerity. These values fuel my desire to help others use their talents and do their best. My experiences as an educator combined with my creative spark and passion for serving others are the essential ingredients in the Creative Outlet Method.

The Creative Outlet Method is the foundation for Joshua's Stage, the nonprofit organization I founded in 2016, whose mission is to enrich the lives of individuals with special needs by providing the opportunity for each participant to demonstrate creativity, develop and maintain self-confidence, and build relationships with peers against the safe and fun backdrop of fine arts, performances, and exhibits.

The Creative Outlet Method seeks to reinforce participants' positive behaviors while decreasing their negative behaviors, using an innovative and unique positive behavior support system. While instructors at Joshua's Stage are trained to implement the Creative Outlet Method, I believe that parents of children with special needs can also successfully conduct theater arts and improv activities using the Creative Outlet Method. Knowing that parents/ primary caregivers can be the strongest influences on a child's growth, you will have the opportunity to make a significantly positive impact on your child's development by using this book. The activities in this book, combined with the

10 components of the Creative Outlet Method, are designed for you to provide opportunities for your child to demonstrate their creativity, increase their self-confidence, and build their social skills. Imagine the moment when you and your child are laughing together because you are performing these activities. Your and your child's creative sparks will shine well into your child's future.

Introduction

While I don't have children with special needs, I can empathize with parents who reveal their stories to me, which often include feelings of frustration, self-doubt, overwhelm, isolation, anxiousness, and utter exhaustion.

Parents share with me that their child's school has little to no idea how to meet their child's needs, or that the ideas that the schools brainstorm are irrelevant to the needs of their child. Many parents and teachers are frustrated by ill-fitting enrichment programs offered by schools. All too frequently I hear from parents that their child was removed from a program because the staff was unable to successfully meet their child's needs.

While parents have no intention of being combative with their child's school, or with the enrichment program, their instinct to protect justifiably kicks in when their child's needs are not being met.

Parents describe the appointments their child endures, such as speech therapy, occupational therapy, physical therapy, applied behavior analysis (ABA) therapy, family therapy, group therapy, in-home therapy, individual therapy, social skills play groups, and the list goes on and on. In addition to therapy appointments, several children take medication for myriad reasons, including anxiety, depression, mood disorders, behavior management, inattention, hyperactivity, and impulsivity.

Do any of these stories or feelings resonate with you? What if your world could be different? What if the frustration, self-doubt, overwhelm, isolation, anxiousness, and utter exhaustion were transformed and manifested itself into something amazing?

Imagine *your* child laughing with friends and family because *you* are doing something unique and innovative with *your* child. *You* are meeting *your* child's needs in a fun, creative, and well-organized play date, birthday party, or family gathering that is child centered.

And the coolest part? You feel alive, energized, and recharged. I can hear it now: "And the parent-of-the-year award goes to . . ." *you*!

Welcome to *The Creative Outlet Method: At-Home Activities for Children with Special Needs*. I am delighted that you are prepared to embark on an exciting journey with your child. My goal is that the ten components of the Creative Outlet Method will teach you to provide your child with opportunities to demonstrate their creativity, increase their self-confidence, and build their social skills.

You will discover the CUPSS (Create, Unique, Positive, Support, Successful) of the Creative Outlet Method, which are the underlying components that helped the method grow into a proven methodology for success. You will have countless opportunities to build your own self-confidence as you encounter the Five Cs (Compassionate, Confident, Creative, Curiosity, Communication) as well as the SOfTS (Serving Others for Tremendous Success) of the Creative Outlet Method. You will enjoy reinforcing your child's positive behaviors, as well as those of their peers and family members, while fostering the HIPPP (Hey, Hey What?! I Am Making Good Decisions. Positive Words. Positive Actions. Participation.) Rules and the A+ Audience Type, both of which are positive behavior supports. With 31 amazingly fun activities prescribed in the Activity Plan Template, you will be able to successfully conduct each activity for your child and their peers and family members in a variety of settings including play dates, birthday parties, family gatherings, and more.

It is my hope that this book will give you the tools to enrich life for you, those around you, and most important, for your child.

Ready? Look at your calendar. Book a play date for your child along with a few of their friends.

Set? Immerse yourself in the Creative Outlet Method and the activities in this book.

Go! Conduct your favorite activities and watch your child shine!

As human beings, our job in life is to help people realize how rare and valuable each one of us really is, that each of us has something that no one else has – or ever will have – something inside that is unique to all time. It's our job to encourage each other to discover that uniqueness and to provide ways of developing its expression.

—**Fred Rogers**

The Creative Outlet Method

The Creative Outlet Method is the process used to enhance every participant's unique abilities while providing them with the opportunity to demonstrate their creativity, increase their self-confidence, and build their social skills.

The HIPPP Rules and the A+ Audience Type are positive behavior supports that I created to help the conductor of the activities manage the participants' behaviors.

While many of the activities in this book are common to theater arts and improv enrichment programs, camps, and schools, embedding the Creative Outlet Method in each activity is the ultimate gateway for you to meet your child's needs.

To foster and maintain a warm and welcoming environment for everyone, successful conductors of the Creative Outlet Method commit to following these 10 components:

1. Implementers and Recipients

2. CUPSS (Create, Unique, Positive, Support, Success)

3. SOfTS (Serving Others for Tremendous Success)

4. RAE of Sunshine Approach (Reflect. Analyze. Engage. Sunshine.)

5. The Five Cs (Compassionate, Confident, Creative, Curiosity, Communication)

6. HIPPP Rules (Hey, Hey What?!, I Am Making Good Decisions, Positive Words, Positive Actions, Participation)

7. Audience Types (A+ Audience, B Audience, Funky Fools)

8. Activity Plans

9. Celebrate Success

10. The Creative Outlet Method Cycle: Each component is defined by what it does and why and how you should use it.

Component 1
Implementers and Recipients

Implementers

Parents – guardians, caregivers, family members

Educators – teachers, administrators, instructional leaders, paraprofessionals

Therapists – psychologists, speech therapists, behavior therapists, occupational therapists

Social workers – family case workers, hospital case workers

Counselors – school, camp, after-school, private practice, group counseling, treatment centers

Coaches – athletic, life, spiritual

Spiritual leaders – pastoral leaders, religious educators

Volunteers – college students, adults, children, senior citizens, volunteer organizations, corporate volunteers

What

Successfully conduct fun activities using the Creative Outlet Method.

Why

Because enriching the lives of individuals with special needs is a rewarding experience.

How

Receive training; follow the 10 components in this book.

Recipients

Individuals with a wide range of special needs – autism, learning disabilities, Down syndrome, emotional disturbance, cognitive delay, cerebral palsy, physical disabilities, speech and language delay, behavior disorder, hearing impairment, vision impairment, and beyond

Typical developing peers – siblings, peer models, friends, community members

> *While professionals in our communities care deeply for their clients, nobody knows your child as well as you do.*

What

Engage in a blast of creativity while experiencing activities enhanced by the Creative Outlet Method.

Why

To demonstrate creativity, increase self-confidence, and build social skills.

How

Participate in fun activities led by implementers of the Creative Outlet Method.

Component 2
CUPSS

Colorful reminders help you, a torch-bearer/implementer of the Creative Outlet Method, to envelop the process on a deeper level.

C	Create	Create and conduct activities with passion for the fine arts
U	Unique	Celebrate everyone's unique abilities while recognizing their accomplishments with the Ferris Wheel Round of Applause
P	Positive	Develop and maintain a positive relationship with everyone
S	Support	Support everyone so that they encourage each other to achieve their best
S	Success	Provide an environment for everyone to feel successful

CUPSS IMPLEMENTERS

What

Create

- Your unique personality will shine as you conduct the activities in this book.

Unique

- The Ferris Wheel Round of Applause.

Positive

- Foster your relationship with your child while you develop a positive rapport with the participants.

Success

- Provide a warm and welcoming environment for the participants.

Why

Create

- The greatest impact on your child's and your child's peers' experiences is influenced by your actions.

Unique

- The Ferris Wheel Round of Applause is designed to simultaneously allow each person to feel good about themselves while congratulating the accomplishments of the performers.

Positive

- Reinforcing positive behaviors decreases the chance for negative behaviors to occur.

Success

- Provide a warm and welcoming environment for the participants.

How

Create

- Perform as a suggested character in several of the activities.

Unique

- Put your right arm up at a 90-degree angle while saying, "Right hand up."

- Put your left arm up at a 90-degree angle while saying, "Left hand up."

- Cross your arms in front of your chest while saying, "Cross 'em front."

- Keeping your arms crossed, use your hands to pat your shoulders while saying, "Pat on the back."

- Do a round of applause, which is applauding while making a big circle with your arms, and say, "Round of applause."

Positive

- Thank your child and the participants for being with you during the activities.

- Let everyone know how much you appreciate them.

Success

- Participants are more likely to engage in the activities when they feel they are in a safe, warm, and welcoming environment.

CUPSS RECIPIENTS

What, Why, How

Support

- Your child and the participants provide each other with verbal praise.

- Strong social skills are essential for positive interactions with others.

- Model good behavior by complimenting participants using the HIPPP Rules and the A+ Audience Type.

- Encourage the participants to compliment each other using the HIPPP Rules.

Component 3
SOfTS – Serving Others for Tremendous Success

We serve each other within our culture of:

Understanding

Patience

Flexibility

Determination

Quality

Humility

Sincerity

Receptiveness

Practice the concepts expressed in the SOfTS and live in a beautiful space to love another person. Think of the people, including yourself, in your child's immediate family. Just as you desire for your child to be successful, you also want to position caregivers to be successful in your child's journey to personal growth and development. Although you and the caregivers may approach your child's behaviors from different points of view, you can develop and maintain setting up your child's team for success with the words expressed in the SOfTS. Your child's community of care will be stronger and more engaging as they benefit from your efforts.

SOfTS Implementers
What, Why, How

- The words that compile the SOfTS.

- Living these words each day will help you feel a sense of fulfillment.

- Loving yourself allows you to serve and love others.

- Daily practices of mindfulness, including meditation, introspection, self-reflection, and physical health.

SOfTS Recipients
What, Why, How

- The words that compile the SOfTS.

- Your child and the participants will appreciate their own unique skills and abilities.

- Your child and the participants will appreciate each other's unique skills and abilities.

- Practicing the HIPPP Rules and engaging in the A+ Audience Type during the activities.

Component 4
RAE of Sunshine Approach

Reflect. Analyze. Engage.
The situation concludes with rays of sunshine.

Your child may exhibit behaviors that cause you to allow yourself feelings of frustration and anger. You want to feel confident and successful when supporting your child's efforts to de-escalate. The RAE of Sunshine Approach is a valuable tool you can immediately implement.

RAE of Sunshine Approach Flow Chart

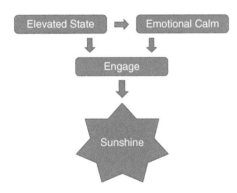

Elevated State

- Your child is demonstrating behavior that is potentially harmful to themselves or to others, or the behavior is prohibiting your child, and/or you, and/or others from accomplishing something.

- Attempting to rationally engage with your child at this stage is difficult.

- Ensuring that you, your child, and others are safe from injury is important. It may be necessary to remove obstacles such as furniture, sharp objects, and fragile belongings out of your child's reach.

- You may need to stand between your child and a door to prevent them from running away.

Calm

- You desire for your child to de-escalate in a safe manner while you maintain your calm.

Engage

- Talking with your child about the impact their behaviors have on themselves and others is essential for their successful growth and development.

Sunshine

- After you have engaged with your child, they can successfully continue with their activities.

Reflect

What do you need to manage your emotions when your child is in an elevated state? Prior to engaging with your child, you will want to reflect, perhaps in just a matter of seconds, on the questions in the following self-assessment:

- How do you feel now?

- Why do you feel this?

- What do you need to do to feel calm?

- Are you willing to take the necessary steps to feel calm?

Recognizing and acknowledging your feelings is important. You will be able to manage your own emotions while you attempt to engage with your child.

Analyze

Check your surroundings while keeping your and your child's safety in mind.

- Is your child safe?

- Are other people in the area safe?

- Are you safe?

- What does your child need at this moment?

Engage

- Remove your child from the situation.

- Ask your child accountable questions using the HIPPP Rules (Hey, Hey What?! I Am Making Good Decisions. Positive Words. Positive Actions. Participation.), for example:

  a. Is hitting me a positive action?

  b. Are the words you are using positive words? Those words hurt my feelings.

  c. Is running away from me a positive action? I want to make sure you are safe.

  d. Is throwing objects at me a positive action? You could hurt me.

- Listen to your child and validate their words and feelings.

- Determine what your child needs, and meet those needs.

- Offer verbal praise to your child as they reach their calm.

Sunshine

- You and your child are at peace.

- Your child's needs have been met.

- Your child can successfully resume their tasks.

Component 5
The Five Cs

C	Compassionate toward others
C	Confident in our work
C	Creative in our approach
C	Curiosity through the eyes of our child
C	Communication with each other

The Five Cs Implementers

Compassionate
What, Why, How

- Kindness toward others.

- Your acts of loving-kindness help others to feel good and to also perform their own acts of loving-kindness.

- Show the participants that you care for their well-being by thanking them for being with you and your child for the activity.

Confident
What, Why, How

- Believe in yourself as you conduct the activities.

- You feel good about yourself.

- Your self-confidence helps your child and the participants to feel

they are in a well-organized and safe environment.

- Review the Activity Plan for each activity that you are conducting in advance, so you are familiar with your role.

- Prepare materials as needed in advance of the activity.

Creative
What, Why, How

- Perform! Have a blast using silly voices and exaggerated movements.

- Your playfulness demonstrates to your child and the participants that you are enjoying yourself, and your child and the participants will understand they have permission to be silly.

- Smile.

- Maintain eye contact.

- Project your voice.

- Make grand movements with your arms.

Curiosity
What, Why, How

- Imagine the positive energy your child and the participants exhibit as they anticipate the fun they are engaging in.

- Engaging in your own playful-ness permits your child and the participants to demonstrate their creativity, increase their self-confidence, and build their social skills.

- Envision the excitement your child and the participants are likely experiencing as you conduct the activities.

- Combine your child's and the participants' positive energy into your own, while sending out your own good vibes.

Communication
What, Why, How

- Engage in meaningful discussion as you interact with your child and the participants throughout the activities.

- Showing that you respect the interests and needs of your child and of the participants supports their creative and emotional growth.

- Ask open-ended questions to gauge the interest level of your child and the participants.

- Actively listen to your child and the participants to understand how they are feeling during the activities.

Component 6
HIPPP Rules

H	Hey, Hey What?!
I	I Am Making Good Decisions
P	Positive Words
P	Positive Actions
P	Participation

Positive Behavioral Interventions and Supports (PBIS) are widely used across schools, classrooms, and enrichment programs. As defined by the Center on Positive Behavioral Interventions and Supports (CPBIS), "PBIS is an evidence-based three-tiered framework to improve and integrate all of the data, systems, and practices affecting student outcomes every day." According to the CPBIS, "The broad purpose of PBIS is to improve the effectiveness, efficiency, and equity of schools and other agencies. PBIS improves social, emotional, and academic outcomes for all students, including students with disabilities and students from under-represented groups."

The practices, principles, and systems that characterize PBIS have been described, studied, and implemented since the early 1960s and 1970s (Carr 2007; Carr et al. 2002; Sugai and Horner 2002). The reauthorization of the Individuals with Disabilities Education Act (IDEA) noted the term "Positive Behavioral Interventions and Supports."

PBIS were employed to minimize disruptive behaviors from all students, including students with disabilities, and to increase expected behaviors. When using PBIS, data is collected to determine the effectiveness of the PBIS program the organization is implementing. For example, when an organization uses PBIS, the number of office referrals in a given time period is tracked and compared to the number of office referrals when PBIS was not applied.

The HIPPP Rules are my innovative approach to replacing language such as, "sit down and be quiet," or "do what I say because I am the adult." Employing the HIPPP Rules reinforces positive behaviors while decreasing the opportunities for negative behaviors to surface. Introducing the HIPPP Rules to your child is one of the activities in this book.

Implementers and Recipients
Hey, Hey What?!
Why

- Fun, positive, and polite approaches to capturing kids' attention provide a significantly better outcome than negative approaches.

How

- Say, "Hey!" to your child and the participants.
- The participants say, "Hey, What?!"

I Am Making Good Decisions

Why

- Fun, positive, and polite approaches to capturing kids' attention provide a significantly better outcome than negative approaches.

How

- Tell your child that you are proud of them for making a good decision.

Positive Words

Why

- Fun, positive, and polite approaches to capturing kids' attention provide a significantly better outcome than negative approaches.

How

- Ask the participants, "Who can give us an example of a positive word?"
- A participant provides an example of a positive word.

Positive Actions

Why

- Fun, positive, and polite approaches to capturing kids' attention provide a significantly better outcome than negative approaches.

How

- Ask the participants, "Who can give us an example of a positive action?"
- A participant provides an example of a positive action.

Participation

Why

- Fun, positive, and polite approaches to capturing kids' attention provide a significantly better outcome than negative approaches.

How

- Ask the participants, "Who can give us an example of participation?"
- A participant provides an example of participation.

Component 7
Audience Types

A+ Audience, B Audience, Funky Fools

A+ Audience	Sitting up straight, eyes and ears open to the person presenting/performing
B Audience	Talking to a neighbor, not really paying attention to the person presenting/performing
Funky Fools	Laughing out loud repeatedly, making noises, not paying any attention to the person presenting/performing

The A+ Audience Type complements the HIPPP Rules. Introducing your child to the Audience Types is one of the activities in this book.

Implementers A+ Audience

What

- The combination of an audience member and a behavior management technique fuses theater arts and positive behavior supports.

Why

- Your child and the participants are motivated to comply with your requests.

- Utilizing the A+ Audience Type countdown is more motivational for your child and participants than demanding that they sit down.

How

- Demonstrate and tell the participants that the A+ Audience Type is: "We're sitting on the floor, our legs are crossed, we're sitting up straight, our eyes are on the person presenting or performing."

B Audience

Why

- Your child and the participants are motivated to comply with your requests.

- The B Audience is inappropriate for the activities.

How

- Demonstrate and tell the participants that the B Audience is: "We're talking to our neighbor, we're looking at our phone, we're chewing our food loudly, and we're not paying attention to the person performing."

Funky Fools

What

- The combination of an audience member and a behavior management technique fuses theater arts and positive behavior supports.

Why

- Your child and the participants are motivated to comply with your requests.

- The Funky Fools audience is inappropriate for the activities.

How

- Demonstrate and tell the participants that Funky Fools is: "The worst kind of audience. We don't ever want to see this audience. Oh no! It's the Funky Fools. What is a Funky Fool? We're on the floor rolling around, laughing, making silly noises, and we're not paying any attention to the person performing."

Component 8

Activity Plans – Activity Plan Template

Each activity in this book is written in an Activity Plan Template. The various components of an activity include elements to best support children with special needs. Each part of the Activity Plan Template is described here.

Activity Name

1. The name of the activity is displayed.

Goal

1. Each activity has a goal for your child to achieve.
2. You strive to help your child and the participants feel successful.
3. The goal answers the question, "What benefit will my child gain from this activity?"
4. Each goal begins with "The goal of the activity is. . ."

Objectives

1. Each activity has three measurable objectives for your child to meet that will support them to achieve the activity's goal.
2. The objectives for each activity focus on

   a. what your child will accomplish to demonstrate creativity
   b. what your child will accomplish to increase self-confidence
   c. what your child will accomplish to build social skills

Materials

1. Several activities include a list of materials you will need to successfully conduct the activity.
2. Materials include items you can likely find in your home, such as a wooden spoon, markers, construction paper, and so forth.
3. In addition, several activities include a supplemental materials list that can be downloaded at [INSERT WEBSITE HERE].
4. The password for accessing the supplemental materials is [INSERT PASSWORD HERE].

Prep Ahead

1. Some of the activities include preparation prior to conducting the activity.
2. Preparation may include arranging furniture, downloading the supplemental materials, and thinking of topics ahead of time.

Notes

1. Several activities include my recommendations on how to implement the activity based on my experiences.

Activity Reminder

The Creative Outlet Method is what makes each activity unique. As a torchbearer of the Creative Outlet Method, you will ignite creativity for the participants. Reminders for each activity are as follows.

1. HIPPP Rules

2. A+ Audience: "A+ back to spots by 3, A+ back to spots by 2, A+ back to spots by 1. Great job! I really like how [say the name of the person] is sitting A+. I also like how [say the name of the person] is sitting A+."

3. "I like how [say the name of the person] is showing [say the component of the HIPPP Rules that the person is exhibiting]."

4. "Hey, Hey What?!"

5. The Ferris Wheel Round of Applause

Facilitator Activity

1. The term *facilitator* is used because you could be a parent, relative, guardian, educator, therapist, or other caregiver.

2. Each activity includes the directions and the scripting for you to follow.

3. You are welcome to adjust the wording of the scripting to best meet the needs of your child and the participants; however, straying too far from the words may alter the activity beyond its purpose.

4. Each step includes the amount of time it may take. While you will frequently see "1 minute" projected, that part of the activity may require less than a minute, or one minute or longer, depending on the needs of your child and the other participants.

Your Child's Activity

1. Each activity includes the steps that your child will perform as they experience the activity.

2. Each step includes the amount of time it may take. While you will frequently see "1 minute" projected, you can expect that part of the activity may require less than a minute, or one minute or longer, depending on the needs of your child and the other participants.

Visual Cues

1. Several activities include visual cues to support your child's experience.

2. Several activities include a list of supplemental materials, which are often the visual cues; this list can be downloaded at [INSERT WEBSITE HERE].

3. The password for accessing the supplemental materials list is [INSERT PASSWORD HERE].

4. Visual cues may also include objects such as a wooden spoon.

Expected Outcomes

1. The expected outcomes are tied to your child's objectives for the activity.

2. If your child accomplishes the objectives, then your child achieved the goal for the activity.

3. Do not worry if your child does not accomplish an objective.

4. Reflect on the activity to determine what can be improved the next time you conduct it.

Component 9

Celebrate Success

You did it! Way to go
Give yourself a Ferris Wheel Round
of Applause!
Right hand up! Left hand up!
Cross 'em in front!
Pat on the back!
Round of applause!

Component 10
The Creative Outlet Method Cycle

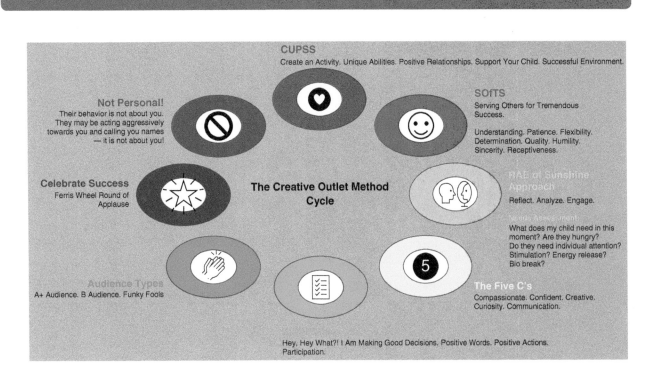

CUPSS
Create an Activity. Unique Abilities. Positive Relationships. Support Your Child. Successful Environment.

Not Personal!
Their behavior is not about you. They may be acting aggressively towards you and calling you names — it is not about you!

SOfTS
Serving Others for Tremendous Success.

Understanding. Patience. Flexibility. Determination. Quality. Humility. Sincerity. Receptiveness.

Celebrate Success
Ferris Wheel Round of Applause

The Creative Outlet Method Cycle

RAE of Sunshine Approach

Reflect. Analyze. Engage.

Needs Assessment
What does my child need in this moment? Are they hungry? Do they need individual attention? Stimulation? Energy release? Bio break?

Audience Types
A+ Audience. B Audience. Funky Fools

The Five C's
Compassionate. Confident. Creative. Curiosity. Communication.

Hey, Hey What?! I Am Making Good Decisions. Positive Words. Positive Actions. Participation.

The Creative Outlet Method Cycle encompasses the CUPSS, the SOfTS, the RAE of Sunshine Approach, the Five Cs, the HIPPP Rules, the Audience Types, Celebrate Success, and a reminder to not take negative behaviors personally. The graphic represents the tools you can implement when your child is demonstrating negative behaviors you would like to see extinguished. You want to praise and encourage your child for exhibiting the behaviors you would like to see continue.

CUPSS

- **Create an activity.** There are over 30 enriching activities in this book that you can conduct for your child and their peers and/or family members.

- **Unique abilities.** Celebrate your child's abilities by reinforcing their strengths and positive behaviors while they experience the activities in this book.

- **Positive relationships.** The activities in this book are designed for you to build your relationship with your child by leading them through the activities while implementing positive behavior supports.

- **Support the participant.** You can support your child during the activities by allowing your child the time they need to engage in the activities and by reinforcing the behaviors you would like them to continue.

- **Successful environment.** In addition to the comfort of your home, you will also create a warm and welcoming environment for your child and for their peers and/or family members while you conduct the activities.

SOFTS

- Serving Others for Tremendous Success. Serving your child and peers and/or family members the gift of creativity is a beautiful act of loving-kindness.

RAE of Sunshine Approach

- Practice self-awareness by checking in with yourself to determine the type of energy you are emitting during your child's behavior episode.

- Analyze – determine if your child is at risk of injuring themself or others during your child's behavior episode.

- Engage – interact with your child using The Creative Outlet Method positive behavior supports and accountable talk.

- Sunshine – when both you and your child are at peace and calm, you can determine that your child is ready to continue participating in the activity.

Needs Assessment

1. What does my child need at this moment?
2. Are they hungry?
3. Do they need individual attention?
4. Stimulation?
5. Energy release?
6. Bathroom break?

The FIVE Cs

- Compassionate toward others

- Confident in our work

- Creative in our approach

- Curiosity through the eyes of our child

- Communication with each other

HIPPP Rules

- You can use the HIPPP Rules to engage your child in accountable talk.

- Hey, Hey What?! Capture your child's attention with a positive and fun proclamation as opposed to something less encouraging such as, "Sit down and be quiet."

- Is that behavior making a good decision? When your child is demonstrating behaviors that you would like to see extinguished, ask your child if the specific behavior is a good decision.

- Are those positive words? When your child is using inappropriate language, ask your child if the words are positive.

- Is that behavior participating in the activity? When your child is demonstrating behaviors that you would like to see extinguished, ask your child if they are participating in the activity.

Audience Types

- A+ Audience – Sitting up straight, eyes and ears open to the person presenting/performing.

- B Audience – Talking to a neighbor, not really paying attention to the person presenting/performing.

- Funky Fools – Laughing out loud repeatedly, making noises, not paying attention to the person presenting/performing.

- You can encourage your child to show you A+ behavior.

Celebrate Success

- **Ferris Wheel Round of Applause –** Right hand up, left hand up, cross

'em in front, pat on the back, and a round of applause!

- The Ferris Wheel Round of Applause should happen after your child and their family members and/or peers perform an activity in this book.

- You can also do the Ferris Wheel Round of Applause with your child when they demonstrate positive and expected behavior in any situation.

Not Personal!

- Your child's behavior is not about you.

- While your child may be calling you names, saying mean things to you, and/or acting physically aggressive toward you, the behavior is not about you.

- Your child is expressing themself through their actions and directing their feelings toward their primary caregiver – you.

- Although the behavior appears personal, the behavior is your child's communication representing your child's needs.

Sample Activities for a One-Hour Session

While the activities in this book are accessible for all ages, you may find it helpful to reference the following *Sample Activities for a One-Hour Session* table. After reviewing the activities in this book, you can decide which activities may work best for your group. To fully immerse yourself, your child, and your guests in the Creative Outlet Method, I strongly encourage you to begin your session with the first six activities noted here and to conclude with Create a Story.

Sequence of Activities	Ages 3 to 5	Ages 6 to 11	Ages 12 to 14	Ages 15 to 18
1	Setting Up the Welcome Circle Audience Types			
2	Ferris Wheel Round of Applause Name Game			
3	Eye Contact Clap Warm-Ups			
4				
5				
6				
7	Follow the Leader		Character Creation	
8	Magical Rocks		Object Transformations	
9	Character Creation	Sour Dough Talk Show	Comic Strip	
10	Hey, Hey What?!	Character Creation	Categories	
11	Animals Alive: Walk, Talk, and Use Chalk		Statues in the Park	
12	Object Transformations			
13	Categories	Categories	Categories	Categories
14	Statues in the Park	Comic Strip	Juice	
15	Juice	Categories	Pizza	
16	Pizza	Statues in the Park	Monologues	
17	Alien Interview	Juice	Yes, And	
18	Imagination Circle	Pizza	Alien Interview	
19	Freeze	Mashed-Up Monologues	Guests at a Party	
20	What's on TV?	Yes, And	What's on TV?	What's for Dinner?
21	What's for Dinner?	Alien Interview	Create a Story	
22	Create a Story			

Activities

Setting Up the Welcome Circle

Goal

To become familiar with the HIPPP Rules and the A+ Audience Type.

Objectives

1. Demonstrate creativity by engaging in relationship-building activities.
2. Increase self-confidence by performing in front of peers.
3. Build social skills by developing relationships with participants.

Materials

HIPPP Rules visual aid

Hey, Hey What?! visual aid

A+ Audience cards

A+ Audience visual aid

Popsicle sticks

Tape

Alliteration cards

Prep Ahead

Review the Activity Plans associated with the Welcome Circle in advance. Set up the materials for the activities as instructed in the Activity Plans.

Notes

The Welcome Circle includes the following activities: HIPPP Rules; Audience Types; Ferris Wheel Round of Applause; Name Game; Eye Contact Clap; Pass the Sound, and Warm-Ups. The Activity Plans for each activity are in the Welcome Circle section of the book. The Activity Reminder references the Creative Outlet Method, and you'll utilize the components after you conduct this introductory activity.

Activity Reminder

Include the Creative Outlet Method components throughout the activity.

1. HIPPP Rules.
2. A+ Audience: "A+ back to spots by 3, A+ back to spots by 2, A+ back to spots by 1. Great job! I really like how [say the name of the person] is sitting A+. I also like how [say the name of the person] is sitting A+."
3. "I like how [say the name of the person] is showing [say the component of the HIPPP Rules that the person is exhibiting]."
4. "Hey, Hey What?!"
5. The Ferris Wheel Round of Applause.

Facilitator Activity

Intro: 1 minute

1. Have everyone sit in a circle on the floor in your designated performance space.

2. Announce, "Welcome to [say your child's name and the gathering you are hosting, i.e. play date, birthday party, family gathering]. I am so glad you all are here with us today. I am excited to have a super-amazing fun time with you all today! Who's ready to have a blast?"

3. Everyone should raise their hands and cheer.

Your Child's Activity

Intro: 1 minute

1. Your child, along with peers and/or family members, sits with you.

Expected Outcomes

Intro

1. Your child feels comfortable, excited, patient, and confident while waiting to perform.

Welcome Circle

HIPPP Rules

Goal

To comprehend the rules of the Creative Outlet Method.

Objectives

1. Demonstrate creativity by identifying examples of the HIPPP Rules.
2. Increase self-confidence by practicing the HIPPP Rules.
3. Build social skills by performing examples of the HIPPP Rules with peers.

Materials

HIPPP Rules visual aid

Hey, Hey What?! visual aid

Prep Ahead

Display the HIPPP Rules visual aid where everyone can see it. Have the Hey, Hey What?! visual aid readily available.

Notes

The HIPPP Rules are the underlying component of the Creative Outlet Method. I created them to serve as a positive behavior support for every participant in every activity. They are the essential elements for celebrating your child and their peers for demonstrating positive behavior.

Facilitator Activity

Hey: 1 minute

1. Have everyone sit in a circle. Point out the HIPPP Rules visual aid and announce, "Who's ready to get HIPPP today? It's time to review our HIPPP Rules. When I say 'Hey' [hold up the Hey, Hey What?! visual aid and show the Hey! side], you say 'Hey what?!'" [hold up the Hey, Hey What?! visual aid and show the Hey, Hey What?! side]
2. Everyone says, "Hey, what?!"
3. Continue, "Hey!" [hold up the Hey, Hey What?! visual aid and show the Hey! side]
4. Gesture to everybody as you hold up the Hey, Hey What?! visual aid and show the Hey, Hey What?! side, and everyone responds, "Hey, what?!"

I am making good decisions: 1 minute

5. Continue, "Great! Who can tell me what the I in the HIPPP Rules stands for?"
6. Someone should volunteer to say, "I am making good decisions."
7. Continue, "That's right! Who can give us an example of making a good decision?"
8. Someone should give an example of making a good decision.

Positive words: 1 minute

9. Continue, "Great! Thank you [name the person who performed the example]. What does the first P in the HIPPP Rules stand for?"

10. Someone should volunteer to say, "Positive words."

11. Continue, "Great! Who can give us an example of a positive word?"

12. Someone should give an example of a positive word.

Positive actions: 1 minute

13. Continue, "Yes! Thank you [say the name of the person who gave the example]. What does the next P in the HIPPP Rules stand for?"

14. Someone should volunteer to say, "Positive actions."

15. Continue, "Great! Who can give us an example of a positive action?"

16. Someone should give an example of a positive action.

Participation: 1 minute

17. Continue, "Wonderful! Thank you [say the name of the person who gave the example]. Everybody, what does the last P in the HIPPP Rules stand for? Let's all say it together."

18. Everyone should say, "Par-ticipation!"

19. Continue, "Great job, everybody! I loved how you all performed our HIPPP Rules! You all HIPPP-ed today! Let's make sure to stay HIPPP all day for our fun activities."

Your Child's Activity

Hey: 1 minute

1. Your child says, "Hey, what?!" when prompted.

I am making good decisions: 1 minute

2. Your child says, "I am making good decisions" when prompted.

3. Your child might give an example of a good decision.

Positive words: 1 minute

4. Your child says, "Positive words" when prompted.

5. Your child might give an example of positive words.

Positive actions: 1 minute

6. Your child says, "Positive actions" when prompted.

7. Your child might give an example of a positive action.

Participation: 1 minute

8. Your child says, "Participation" when prompted.

Visual Cues

HIPPP Rules visual aid

Hey, Hey What?! visual aid

Expected Outcomes

1. Your child demonstrates creativity by identifying examples of the HIPPP Rules.

2. Your child increases self-confidence by practicing the HIPPP Rules.

3. Your child builds social skills by performing examples of the HIPPP Rules with peers.

Welcome Circle

Audience Types

Goal

To demonstrate respect for the person(s) speaking and/or performing.

Objectives

1. Demonstrate positive behavior by performing a respectful posture.
2. Increase self-confidence to feel good for respecting others.
3. Build social skills by showing respect when others perform and speak.

Materials

A+ Audience cards

A+ Audience visual aid

Popsicle sticks

Tape

Prep Ahead

Cut out the A+ Audience cards and tape them to the popsicle sticks so there are enough for each participant. Have the A+ Audience visual aid readily available.

Notes

My A+ Audience concept serves two purposes. The first is a behavior management component to support participants during activities so that they return to their designated spots in an orderly manner, without having to shout things like, "Back to your spots!" or "Sit down!" The second is a prompt to demonstrate appropriate behavior during a theatrical performance, i.e. sitting up straight, eyes on the person presenting, and ears open listening to the person presenting.

Facilitator Activity

Intro: 1 minute

1. Have everyone seated in the circle.
2. Ask, "Who has been to a show? A performance? Where people are on stage? When you are watching the people on stage, what are you a part of?"
3. Participants should eventually answer that they are part of the audience.
4. Continue, "Right! You are part of the audience. When you are in the audience, do you sit quietly and watch the performance, or do you make noise and disrupt others?"
5. Participants should answer that they sit quietly and watch the performance.
6. Continue, "Today I am going to show you three different audience types."

A+ Audience: 1 minute

7. Distribute the A+ Audience cards to the participants so that everyone has one.

8. Announce, "The first type of audience is the best type of audience that is, and that ever will be. It's called the A+ Audience."

9. Hold up your A+ Audience card and the A+ Audience visual aid.

10. Continue, "For the A+ Audience, the audience type I expect you to do at all times, we're sitting on the floor, our legs are crossed, we're sitting up straight, our eyes are on the person presenting or performing, and right now that person is me, and our ears are listening to that person, and right now that person is me."

11. Everyone should be sitting A+.

12. Continue, "Great job A+!"

B Audience: 1 minute

13. Announce, "The second Audience type is the B Audience. In the B Audience we're talking to our neighbor, we're looking at our phone, we're chewing our food loudly, we're not paying attention to the person performing. Here's what the B Audience looks like."

14. Lean in next to your child and pretend to whisper in their ear, point at something far away, and start to quietly laugh.

15. Announce, "Now you try. B Audience, go!"

16. Everyone should be practicing being the B Audience.

17. Announce, "Hey!"

18. Everyone else, "Hey, what?!"

19. Hold up the A+ Audience visual aid and your A+ Audience card.

20. Announce, "Back to A+ by 3, A+ by 2, A+ by 1. Good job!"

21. Everyone should be sitting in the A+ position.

Funky Fools: 1 minute

22. Announce, "The third type of audience is the worst kind of audience. We don't ever want to see this audience. Oh no! It's the Funky Fools. What is a Funky Fool? We're on the floor rolling around, laughing, making silly noises, and we're not paying any attention to the person performing. Here's what the Funky Fool looks like."

23. Roll around on the floor, laugh loudly, and make silly noises.

24. Announce, "Now you try. Funky Fools, go!"

25. Everyone should be practicing being a Funky Fool.

26. Announce, "Hey!"

27. Everyone else, "Hey, what?!"

28. Hold up the A+ Audience visual aid and your A+ Audience card.

29. Announce, "Back to A+ by 3, A+ by 2, A+ by 1. Good job!"

30. Everyone should be sitting in the A+ position.

Your Child's Activity

Intro: 1 minute

1. Your child participates in the discussion about being a member of the audience.

A+ Audience: 1 minute

2. Your child performs the A+ Audience.

B Audience: 1 minute

3. Your child performs the B Audience type followed by the A+ Audience type.

Funky Fools: 1 minute

4. Your child performs the Funky Fools Audience type followed by the A+ Audience type.

Visual Cues

A+ Audience card

A+ Audience visual aid

Expected Outcomes

Intro

1. Your child feels comfortable, excited, patient, and confident while waiting to perform.

A+ Audience, B Audience, Funky Fools

2. Your child demonstrates creativity by performing a respectful posture.

3. Your child increases self-confidence by feeling good for respecting others.

4. Your child builds social skills by showing respect for others as they perform and speak.

Welcome Circle
Ferris Wheel Round of Applause

Goal
To praise oneself and peers.

Objectives
1. Demonstrate creativity by making celebratory movements.
2. Increase self-confidence by performing with peers.
3. Build social skills by celebrating peers' accomplishments.

Facilitator Activity

Intro: 1 minute

1. Have everyone sit or stand in a circle.
2. Announce, "To make sure our friends know how proud we are of them when they perform, we are going to do the Ferris Wheel Round of Applause."

Ferris Wheel Round of Applause: 1 minute

3. Put your right arm up at a 90-degree angle while saying, "Right hand up."
4. Put your left arm up at a 90-degree angle while saying, "Left hand up."
5. Cross your arms in front of your chest while saying, "Cross 'em front."
6. Keeping your arms crossed, use your hands to pat your shoulders while saying, "Pat on the back."
7. Do a round of applause, which is applauding while making a big circle with your arms and say, "Round of applause."

Your Child's Activity

Intro: 1 minute

1. Your child, along with peers and/or family members, stands or sits with you.

Ferris Wheel Round of Applause: 1 minute

2. Your child follows your movements and statements while performing the Ferris Wheel Round of Applause.

Expected Outcomes

Intro

1. Your child feels comfortable, excited, patient, and confident while waiting to perform.

Ferris Wheel Round of Applause

2. Your child demonstrates creativity by making celebratory movements.
3. Your child increases self-confidence by performing with peers.
4. Your child builds social skills by celebrating peers' accomplishments.

Welcome Circle

Name Game

Goal

To learn the names of the other participants.

Objectives

1. Demonstrate creativity by performing movements associated with your child's name.
2. Increase self-confidence by performing for peers.
3. Build social skills by waiting to take a turn.

Notes

The Name Game is frequently played as an icebreaker at various events. The Name Game is a perfect game for the beginning of your event.

Facilitator Activity

Welcome: 1 minute

1. Welcome everyone and share how excited you are for your child and peers and/or family members to perform for everyone.

Intro: 1 minute

2. Have everyone stand in a circle.
3. Announce, "Let's get to know each other's names by playing a fun game. We'll go around the circle and have each person say their name and do a movement. Then, we'll say that person's name and do their movement. I'll go first."
4. Say your name out loud and do something like jumping up and turning around. Gesture for everyone else to say your name and do the same movement.
5. Have your child go next.

Name Game: 3 minutes

6. Have each participant say their name and perform a movement, with everyone repeating the name and performing the movement.

Your Child's Activity

Welcome: 1 minute

1. Your child, along with peers and/or family members, stands with you.

Intro: 1 minute

2. Your child says your name and repeats your movement.
3. Your child says their name and performs a movement.

Expected Outcomes

Welcome

1. Your child feels comfortable, excited, patient, and confident while waiting to perform.

Name Game

1. Your child demonstrates creativity by performing movements associated with peers' names.

2. Your child increases self-confidence by performing for peers.

3. Your child builds social skills by waiting to take a turn.

Welcome Circle

Eye Contact Clap

Goal

To increase your child's self-awareness.

Objectives

1. Demonstrate creativity by making sounds and movements.
2. Increase self-confidence by engaging in an activity with peers.
3. Build social skills by maintaining self-awareness of personal space and the personal space of peers.

Notes

The first time I watched someone conduct Eye Contact Clap, I knew right away that the activity is designed as a fantastic approach for participants to get to know each other in a fun and nonthreatening manner. For participants who tend to hit others when frustrated, Eye Contact Clap reinforces the idea that physical contact can be fun when directed appropriately, as opposed to exhibiting physical aggression.

Facilitator Activity

Intro: 1 minute

1. While sitting in the Welcome Circle, announce, "I see that everyone is doing a great job sitting A+. To make sure we have a lot of fun today, we need to get focused. Who's ready to have fun and focus? Let's start a beat."

2. Open your hands, palms down, and pat your lap loud enough so everyone can hear the sound. You'll be keeping a beat to the chant *Eye Contact Clap*. Once you have the beat going, ask everyone to join you.

3. Once everyone is patting their laps along with your beat, announce, "Great job keeping the beat. Join me in saying 'Eye Contact Clap.'"

4. As everyone joins in, continue to explain the activity while you are keeping the beat: "In just a moment we'll start getting focused. I am going to turn to the person next to me [say the name of your child], and when I get to the word *contact,* I will turn my body to [their name] and we will make eye contact, and we will clap each other's hands on the word *clap*. As we do that, everyone should keep the beat going and continue to say, "Eye Contact Clap." We'll have everyone make eye contact and clap hands through the circle."

Eye Contact Clap: 3 minutes

5. Continue to lead everyone in keeping a beat while chanting "Eye Contact Clap," and help participants as needed to make eye contact and clap hands with each other.

Eye Contact Clap enhancements: 3 minutes

6. Make the beat go faster each time around the circle.

7. Make the beat go slower each time around the circle.

8. Make the chant a whisper each time around the circle.

Conclusion: 1 minute

9. After about 3 minutes, conclude the activity with everyone doing a round of applause.

Your Child's Activity

Intro: 1 minute

1. Your child, along with peers and/or family members, sits in the circle.

Eye Contact Clap: 3 minutes

2. Your child chants and keeps a beat to *Eye Contact Clap* while making eye contact and clapping hands with you and the other person next to them.

Eye Contact Clap enhancements: 3 minutes

3. Your child chants and keeps a beat to *Eye Contact Clap* while making eye contact and clapping hands with you and the other person next to them.

Conclusion: 1 minute

4. Your child performs a round of applause with peers.

Expected Outcomes

Intro

1. Your child feels comfortable, excited, patient, and confident while waiting to perform.

Eye Contact Clap and enhancements

2. Your child demonstrates creativity by making sounds and movements.

3. Your child increases self-confidence by engaging in the activity with peers.

4. Your child builds social skills by maintaining self-awareness of personal space and the personal space of others.

Conclusion

5. Your child increases self-confidence while performing with peers.

Welcome Circle

Pass the Sound

Goal

To perform by creating sounds.

Objectives

1. Demonstrate creativity by making unique sounds.
2. Increase self-confidence by performing with peers.
3. Build social skills by waiting for a turn.

Prep Ahead

Depending on your comfort level with improvising, you may want to have a couple of silly sounds in mind before the activity.

Notes

Pass the Sound permits you and the participants to create silliness while feeling confident.

Facilitator Activity

Intro: 1 minute

1. While everyone is sitting in the circle, look at the top of your child's head.
2. While pointing to the top of your child's head, announce, "Oh my, do you see it? Does everybody see that? Look what's on your head!"

3. Pretend to pick up a small object from your child's head.
4. Continue, "I have it. I have a sound. I need to hear the sound. Hold on, everyone."
5. Bring your hand to your ear and make a silly face.
6. Continue, "Oh wow. What a sound. I am going to pass this sound and then everyone will pass it to the person next to them. Here we go."

Part 1: 2 minutes

7. Open your hand and pretend to throw a small object to your child while making the silly sound.
8. Your child makes the same silly sound to the person next to them while pretending to throw the sound to the person next to them.
9. The game continues until the last person passes the sound back to you.

Part 2: 2 minutes

10. While pointing to the top of your child's head, announce, "Oh my, do you see it? Does everybody see that? Look what's on your head!"
11. Pretend to pick up a small object from your child's head.
12. Continue, "I have it. I have a sound. I need to hear the sound. Hold on, everyone."

13. Bring your hand to your ear and make a silly face.

14. Continue, "Oh wow. What a sound. This time I am going to pass this sound to someone and then that person will catch the sound. Then that person will pass it to the person next to them and they will catch it. Let's practice."

15. Pass the sound to your child, and have your child catch the sound by opening their hands, slowly closing their hands over the sound, bringing their hands into their chest, and making the sound backward.

16. Then have your child pass the sound to the person next to them, and that person will catch it in the same way your child caught the sound.

17. The game continues until the last person passes the sound back to you, and you catch it.

Your Child's Activity

Intro: 1 minute

1. Your child, along with peers and/or family members, sits with you in the circle.

Part 1: 2 minutes

2. Your child makes your sound and passes it to the person next to them.

Part 2: 2 minutes

3. Your child makes your sound and passes it to the person next to them.

4. Your child catches the sound when their peer passes the sound to them.

Expected Outcomes

Intro

1. Your child feels comfortable, excited, patient, and confident while waiting to perform.

Part 1 and Part 2

2. Your child demonstrates creativity by making unique sounds.

3. Your child increases self-confidence by performing with peers.

4. Your child builds social skills by waiting for their turn.

Welcome Circle

Warm-Ups

Goal

To stimulate your child's creative energy.

Objectives

1. Demonstrate creativity by making sounds associated with words and characters.
2. Increase self-confidence by leading peers.
3. Build social skills by following a leader and by being the leader.

Materials

Alliteration cards

Popsicle sticks

Tape

Prep Ahead

Cut out the alliteration cards and tape them to the popsicle sticks so there are enough for each participant to have a complete set.

Notes

As I was conducting activities in the Welcome Circle, I recognized that having an activity that included something tangible for the participants would be valuable. The alliteration cards are fabulous items for participants to hold while they are pronouncing sounds and words. I know you will see their value as well.

Facilitator Activity

Intro: 1 minute

1. While sitting in the Welcome Circle, announce, "I see that everyone is doing a great job sitting A+. So that we can do our best job performing, we are going to have fun warming up."
2. Distribute a set of alliteration cards to each participant.
3. Continue, "We'll be taking these cool cards and saying some fun sound words. Let's begin."

Boom: 1 minute

4. Have everyone pick up their Boom alliteration card, including you.
5. Move the Boom alliteration card back and forth as you say, "Boo, boo, boom, boom, boo, boo."
6. Gesture to everyone and say, "Join me. Boo, boo, boom, boom, boo, boo."
7. Continue, "That was a great job. Who would like to lead us in our Boom warm-up?"
8. Call on your child to lead the Boom warm-up.
9. Everyone follows along with your child.

Canary: 1 minute

10. Have everyone pick up their Bird alliteration card, including you.

11. Move the Bird alliteration card back and forth as you say, "Kah, kah, canary, canary, kah, kah."

12. Gesture to everyone and say, "Kah, kah, canary, canary, kah, kah."

13. Continue, "That was a great job. Who would like to lead us in our Canary warm-up?"

14. Call on a participant to lead the Canary warm-up.

15. Everyone follows along with the participant.

Messy: 1 minute

16. Have everyone pick up their Messy Kid alliteration card, including you.

17. Move the Messy Kid alliteration card back and forth as you say, "Meh, meh, messy, messy, meh, meh."

18. Gesture to everyone and say, "Meh, meh, messy, messy, meh, meh."

19. Continue, "That was a great job. Who would like to lead us in our Messy warm-up?"

20. Call on a participant to lead the Messy warm-up.

21. Everyone follows along with the participant.

Super: 1 minute

22. Have everyone pick up their Super alliteration card, including you.

23. Move the Super alliteration card back and forth as you say, "Sss, sss, super, super, sss, sss."

24. Gesture to everyone and say, "Sss, sss, super, super, sss, sss."

25. Continue, "That was a great job. Who would like to lead us in our Super warm-up?"

26. Call on a participant to lead the Super warm-up.

27. Everyone follows along with the participant.

Watch: 1 minute

28. Have everyone pick up their Watch alliteration card, including you.

29. Move the Watch alliteration card back and forth as you say, "Waw, waw, Watch, Watch, waw, waw."

30. Gesture to everyone and say, "Waw, waw, Watch, Watch, waw, waw."

31. Continue, "That was a great job. Who would like to lead us in our Watch warm-up?"

32. Call on a participant to lead the Watch warm-up.

33. Everyone follows along with the participant.

34. Tell everyone they did a great job with the vocal warm-ups, and lead everyone in a round of applause.

35. Have everyone stand up as you say, "Join me as we get our bodies ready for performing."

Body shake-outs on 5-count: 2 minutes

36. Raise your right arm straight above your head, and shake it as you say, "Everyone, right arm up in the air, and say, 'Hello ceiling.'"

37. Everyone says, "Hello ceiling."

38. Shake your arm as you say, "Shake it on 1, 2, 3, 4, 5."

39. Lower your right arm and raise your left arm straight above your head, and shake it as you say, "Everyone, left arm up in the air, and say, 'Hello ceiling.'"

40. Everyone says, "Hello ceiling."

41. Shake your arm as you say, "Shake it on 1, 2, 3, 4, 5."

42. Lower your left arm and extend your right leg straight out, and shake it as you say, "Everyone, right leg out, and say, 'Hello floor.'"

43. Everyone says, "Hello floor."

44. Shake your leg as you say, "Shake it on 1, 2, 3, 4, 5."

45. Lower your right leg and extend your left leg straight out, and shake it as you say, "Everyone, left leg out, and say, 'Hello floor.'"

46. Everyone says, "Hello floor."

47. Shake your leg as you say, "Shake it on 1, 2, 3, 4, 5."

Body shake-outs on 3-count: 2 minutes

48. Raise your right arm straight above your head, and shake it as you say, "Everyone, right arm up in the air, and say, 'Hello ceiling.'"

49. Everyone says, "Hello ceiling."

50. Shake your arm as you say, "Shake it on 1, 2, 3."

51. Lower your right arm and raise your left arm straight above your head, and shake it as you say, "Everyone, left arm up in the air, and say, 'Hello ceiling.'"

52. Everyone says, "Hello ceiling."

53. Shake your arm as you say, "Shake it on 1, 2, 3."

54. Lower your left arm and extend your right leg straight out, and shake it as you say, "Everyone, right leg out, and say, 'Hello floor.'"

55. Everyone says, "Hello floor."

56. Shake your leg as you say, "Shake it on 1, 2, 3."

57. Lower your right leg and extend your left leg straight out, and shake it as you say, "Everyone, left leg out, and say, 'Hello floor.'"

58. Everyone says, "Hello floor."

59. Shake your leg as you say, "Shake it on 1, 2, 3."

Body shake-outs on 1-count: 2 minutes

60. Raise your right arm straight above your head, and shake it as you say, "Everyone, right arm up in the air, and say, 'Hello ceiling.'"

61. Everyone says, "Hello ceiling."

62. Shake your arm as you say, "Shake it on 1."

63. Lower your right arm and raise your left arm straight above your head, and shake it as you say, "Everyone, left arm up in the air, and say, 'Hello ceiling.'"

64. Everyone says, "Hello ceiling."

65. Shake your arm as you say, "Shake it on 1."

66. Lower your left arm and extend your right leg straight out, and shake it as you say, "Everyone, right leg out, and say, 'Hello floor.'"

67. Everyone says, "Hello floor."

68. Shake your leg as you say, "Shake it on 1."

69. Lower your right leg and extend your left leg straight out, and shake it as you say, "Everyone, left leg out, and say, 'Hello floor.'"

70. Everyone says, "Hello floor."

71. Shake your leg as you say, "Shake it on 1."

Conclusion: 1 minute

72. Conclude the activity with everyone doing a round of applause.

Your Child's Activity

Boom: 1 minute

1. Your child follows along with you during the Boom warm-up.

2. Your child leads everyone in the Boom warm-up.

Canary: 1 minute

3. Your child follows along with you during the Canary warm-up.

Messy: 1 minute

4. Your child follows along with you during the Messy warm-up.

Super: 1 minute

5. Your child follows along with you during the Super warm-up.

Watch: 1 minute

6. Your child follows along with you during the Waw warm-up.

Transition: 1 minute

7. Your child, along with peers and/or family members, applauds, and stands up.

Body shake-outs on 5-count, 3-count, and 1-count: 2 minutes

8. Your child follows along with your body shake-outs.

Conclusion: 1 minute

9. Your child performs a round of applause with peers.

Visual Cues

Boom alliteration card, Bird alliteration card, Messy Kid alliteration card,

Super alliteration card, Watch alliteration card

Expected Outcomes

Boom, Canary, Messy, Super, and Watch

1. Your child demonstrates creativity by making sounds associated with words and characters.

2. Your child increases self-confidence by leading peers.

3. Your child builds social skills by following a leader and by being the leader.

Transition

4. Your child feels comfortable, excited, patient, and confident while waiting to perform.

Body shake-outs on 5-count, 3-count, and 1-count

5. Your child demonstrates creativity by making movements.

6. Your child increases self-confidence by following along with peers.

7. Your child builds social skills by following a leader.

Conclusion

8. Your child increases self-confidence while performing with peers.

Sourdough Talk Show

Goal

To perform the leading role in a scene.

Objectives

1. Demonstrate creativity by performing a character during the entire scene.

2. Increase self-confidence by performing for the entire scene.

3. Build social skills by taking turns with peers and/or family members three out of three times.

Materials

Character cards

Three chairs

Microphone prop: examples include a wooden spoon, a whisk, a spatula

Solid-colored tape

Costumes (optional)

Prep Ahead

In your designated performance space, set up three chairs facing the audience. The performers put on their costumes (if using) and they wear their character cards. Provide the microphone prop to your child. Write the name of each guest character on a piece of solid-colored tape and place each piece of tape on the top of a chair.

Notes

Sourdough Talk Show is one of my own activities. Your child and peers and/or family members are encouraged to practice the scene prior to the performance. You can support non-readers by prompting them with their lines.

Activity Reminder

Include the Creative Outlet Method components throughout the activity.

1. HIPPP Rules.

2. A+ Audience: "A+ back to spots by 3, A+ back to spots by 2, A+ back to spots by 1. Great job! I really like how [say the name of the person] is sitting A+. I also like how [say the name of the person] is sitting A+."

3. "I like how [say the name of the person] is showing [say the component of the HIPPP Rules that the person is exhibiting]."

4. "Hey, Hey What?!"

5. The Ferris Wheel Round of Applause.

Facilitator Activity

Welcome: 1 minute

Welcome everyone and share how excited you are for your child and peers and/or family members to perform for everyone.

Intro: 1 minute

Announce, "Ladies and gentlemen, give a round of applause for our performers. We have Bobo played by [say name of person playing Bobo]. We have Jackie played by [say name of person playing Jackie]. We have Jenny played by [say name of person playing Jenny]. And we have Toast played by [say name of your child]. Let the show begin!"

Performance: 2 minutes

The performers begin the show.

Performance Conclusion: 1 minute

Gesture for the performers to stand in a line facing the audience. Lead the performers in taking a bow.

Your Child's Activity

Welcome: 1 minute

1. Your child, along with peers and/or family members, stands with you.

Intro: 1 minute

2. Your child's peers and/or family members sit in their assigned chairs.

3. Your child stands next to one of the characters on either end.

4. Each performer waves to the audience as they hear their name.

Performance: 2 minutes

5. Your child begins the show by performing their role as Toast.

6. Your child continues to perform their role as Toast throughout the remainder of the performance.

Performance Conclusion: 1 minute

7. Your child and peers and/or their family members bow for the audience.

Visual Cues

Character cards

Chairs

Microphone prop

Solid-colored tape

Costumes (if using)

Expected Outcomes

Welcome and Intro

1. Your child feels comfortable, excited, patient, and confident while waiting to perform.

Performance

2. Your child demonstrates creativity by performing in the role of Toast for the entire scene.

3. Your child increases self-confidence while performing for an audience.

4. Your child builds social skills while practicing turn-taking during the entire scene.

Performance Conclusion

5. Your child increases self-confidence while performing for an audience.

Animals Alive
Walk, Talk, and Use Chalk

Goal

To perform the leading role in a scene.

Objectives

1. Demonstrate creativity by performing a character during the entire scene.

2. Increase self-confidence by performing the entire scene for an audience.

3. Build social skills by taking turns with peers and/or family members three out of three times.

Materials

Character cards

Three chairs

Microphone prop: examples include a wooden spoon, a whisk, a spatula

Solid-colored tape

Costumes (optional)

Chalk

Black construction paper

Prep Ahead

Have each child draw their character using the chalk on the black construction paper. Display the drawings in your designated performance space. In your designated performance space, set up three chairs facing the audience. The performers put on their costumes (if using), and wear their character cards. Provide the microphone prop to your child. Write the name of each guest character on a piece of solid-colored tape and place each piece of tape on the top of a chair.

Notes

Animals Alive: Walk, Talk, and Use Chalk is my own version of theater games involving animal traits. Your child and peers and/or family members are encouraged to practice the scene prior to the performance. Work with your child on directing the characters to move around according to the script. You can support non-readers by having them perform animal sounds and movements.

Activity Reminder

Include the Creative Outlet Method components throughout the activity.

1. HIPPP Rules.

2. A+ Audience: "A+ back to spots by 3, A+ back to spots by 2, A+ back to spots by 1. Great job! I really like how [say the name of the person] is sitting A+. I also like how [say the name of the person] is sitting A+."

3. "I like how [say the name of the person] is showing [say the component of the HIPPP Rules that the person is exhibiting]."

4. "Hey, Hey What?!"
5. The Ferris Wheel Round of Applause.

Facilitator Activity

Welcome: 1 minute

1. Welcome everyone and share how excited you are for your child and peers and/or family members to perform for everyone.

Intro: 1 minute

2. Announce, "Ladies and gentlemen, give a round of applause for our performers. We have Pana-momma Llama played by [say name of person playing Pana-momma Llama]. We have Bow-Wow Chicka-Chicka Cow-Cow played by [say name of person playing Bow-Wow Chicka-Chicka Cow-Cow]. We have Monday Monty Monkey played by [say name of person playing Monday Monty Monkey]. And we have Toast played by [say name of your child]. Let the show begin!"

Performance: 3 minutes

3. The performers begin the show.

Performance Conclusion: 1 minute

4. Gesture for the performers to stand in a line facing the audience. Lead the performers in taking a bow.

Your Child's Activity

Welcome: 1 minute

1. Your child, along with peers and/or family members, stands with you.

Intro: 1 minute

2. Your child's peers and/or family members sit in their assigned chairs.
3. Your child stands next to one of the characters on either end.
4. Each performer waves to the audience as they hear their name.

Performance: 2 minutes

5. Your child begins the show by performing the role of Toast.
6. Your child continues to perform the role of Toast throughout the remainder of the performance.

7. Your child and their peers and/or family members bow for the audience.

Visual Cues

Character cards

Microphone prop

Solid-colored tape

Costumes (if using)

Chalk

Black construction paper

Expected Outcomes

Welcome and Intro

1. Your child feels comfortable, excited, patient, and confident while waiting to perform.

Performance

2. Your child demonstrates creativity by performing in the role of Toast for the entire scene.

3. Your child increases self-confidence while performing for an audience.

4. Your child builds social skills while practicing turn-taking during the entire scene.

Follow the Leader

Goal

To build leadership and nonverbal communication skills.

Objectives

1. Create movements that can be followed by others.

2. Increase self-confidence while performing the role of the group leader.

3. Build social skills by taking turns and following a leader.

Notes

I am always impressed when I conduct this version of Follow the Leader as the participants quickly engage in the game.

Activity Reminder

Include the Creative Outlet Method components throughout the activity.

1. HIPPP Rules.

2. A+ Audience: "A+ back to spots by 3, A+ back to spots by 2, A+ back to spots by 1. Great job! I really like how [say the name of the person] is sitting A+. I also like how [say the name of the person] is sitting A+."

3. "I like how [say the name of the person] is showing [say the component of the HIPPP Rules that the person is exhibiting]."

4. "Hey, Hey What?!"

5. The Ferris Wheel Round of Applause.

Facilitator Activity

Welcome: 1 minute

1. Welcome everyone and share how excited you are for your child and peers and/or family members to play a game together.

Intro: 2 minutes

2. Have everyone sit in a circle.

3. You are the leader for the opening part of the game.

4. Tell everyone that the leader of the group creates movements without making sounds, and that everyone copies your movements.

5. Everyone copies your movements.

6. Tell everyone that in the next round there will be a new leader and a guesser.

7. Explain that the guesser will turn away from the circle until a new leader is chosen. When a new leader begins moving, explain that you will ask the guesser to turn around and see if they can guess who is leading the group.

8. After about a minute, ask if someone would like to be the guesser for the next round.

Round 1: The Leader: 1 minute

9. Ask the guesser to face the other way in the circle.

10. Ask who would like to be the leader. You can point to your child to be the leader.

11. Explain to the group that you will ask the person volunteering to be the leader to nod their head up and down for "yes," they want to be the leader, or they can shake it side-to-side for "no," they do not want to be the leader.

12. Point to the leader – your child – and say, "Okay everyone, this is our leader. Leader, are you ready? You can answer by nodding your head up and down."

13. Once the leader acknowledges that they are ready, let the leader know that they can begin leading the group by making movements.

Round 1: The Guesser: 1 minute

14. Once the group is following the movements of the leader, ask the guesser to turn around and join the circle.

15. Ask the guesser to try to figure out who is the leader.

16. The guesser can point to the person they think the leader is.

17. Once the guesser correctly identifies the leader, have everyone applaud for the leader and the guesser.

18. Ask who would like to be the guesser for the next round.

Rounds 2 and Beyond: 5–7 minutes

19. Continue the previous steps for the next several rounds.

Conclusion: 1 minute

20. Gesture for the performers to stand in a line facing the audience. Lead the performers in taking a bow.

Your Child's Activity

Welcome: 1 minute

1. Your child, along with peers and/or family members, stands with you.

Intro: 2 minutes

2. Your child follows your movements.

Round 1: The Leader: 1 minute

3. Your child creates movements.

Round 1:– The Guesser: 1 minute

4. Your child creates movements.

Conclusion

5. Your child and peers and/or family members bow for the audience.

Expected Outcomes

Welcome

1. Your child feels comfortable, excited, patient, and confident while waiting to play the game.

Intro

2. Your child builds social skills by copying the movements of the leader.

Round 1: The Leader and the Guesser

3. Your child creates movements, without making sounds, that everyone else was able to follow.

4. Your child feels confident while performing the role of the group leader.

Conclusion

5. Your child increases self-confidence while performing for an audience.

Magical Rocks

Goal

To demonstrate creativity by participating with peers.

Objectives

1. Demonstrate creativity by performing as a character/object during the entire scene.
2. To increase self-confidence by performing the entire scene with peers.
3. To build social skills by taking turns with peers and/or family members three out of three times.

Prep Ahead

Think of objects and animals that your child can perform as, such as: trees, airplanes, rocket ships, jungle animals, farm animals, race car drivers, dinosaurs, car washers, firefighters, pizza makers, and more imaginative ideas such as purple unicorns riding to the castle, a monster with 10 arms, a flying fish eating a broccoli sandwich, a motorcycle powered by orange juice and chocolate, and so on.

Notes

The first time I watched Magical Rocks take place, I knew it would be a lot of fun for all ages. For older participants, you can increase the complexity of the magic rock changes.

Activity Reminder

Include the Creative Outlet Method components throughout the activity.

1. HIPPP Rules.
2. A+ Audience: "A+ back to spots by 3, A+ back to spots by 2, A+ back to spots by 1. Great job! I really like how [say the name of the person] is sitting A+. I also like how [say the name of the person] is sitting A+."
3. "I like how [say the name of the person] is showing [say the component of the HIPPP Rules that the person is exhibiting]."
4. "Hey, Hey What?!"
5. The Ferris Wheel Round of Applause.

Facilitator Activity

Welcome: 1 minute

1. Welcome everyone and share how excited you are for your child and their peers and/or family members to play a game together.

Intro: 2 minutes

2. Have everyone sit in a circle.
3. Announce, "Magical rocks by 3 . . . by 2 . . . by 1."
4. As you are announcing, you get into the magical rock position, in which you kneel and tuck in like a ball. Have the participants get into the magical rock position.

Part 1: 1 minute

5. From your magical rock position, announce, "We are now magical rocks. As we come out of magical rocks, we are turning into trees."

6. As you are announcing, you slowly stand up and position your body so that you are standing like a tree.

7. "Here comes the wind, let's all sway to the left. Here comes more wind, blowing us to the right, now forward, and backward."

8. You act like you are a tree swaying in the wind. Make sure that everyone is swaying like a tree in the wind.

Part 2: 1 minute

9. After everyone seems content with being a tree swaying in the wind, announce, "Back to magical rocks by 3 . . . by 2 . . . by 1."

10. As you are announcing you get into the magical rock position, in which you kneel and tuck in.

Part 3: 1 minute

11. From your magical rock position, announce, "As we come out of magical rocks, we are turning into [one of the ideas mentioned in the **Prep Ahead** section]."

12. As you are announcing, you slowly position your body so that you are representing one of the ideas mentioned in the **Prep Ahead** section, or one of your own ideas.

13. Announce how everyone should move like that character/object.

Conclusion: 3 minutes

14. Continue with the preceding steps, using different ideas.

Your Child's Activity

Welcome: 1 minute

1. Your child, along with peers and/or family members, stands with you.

Intro: 1 minute

2. Your child follows your lead, sits in the circle, and starts turning into a magical rock.

Parts 1, 2, and 3: 1 minute each

3. Your child follows your lead and starts turning into the designated character/object.

Conclusion: 3 minutes

4. Your child follows your lead and starts turning into the designated character/object.

Visual Cues
Expected Outcomes

Welcome and Intro

1. Your child feels comfortable, excited, patient, and confident while waiting to play the game.

Parts 1, 2, 3, and Conclusion

2. Your child demonstrates creativity by performing as a character/object for the entire scene.

3. Your child increases self-confidence by performing the entire scene with peers.

4. Your child builds social skills by taking turns.

Character Creation

Goal

To create and perform a unique character.

Objectives

1. Create a character with little to no prompting.
2. Illustrate their character without support.
3. Perform as the character.

Materials

Character template printed on cardstock

Markers

Crayon

Yarn

Scissors

Googly eyes stickers

Glue

Premade character made on card stock

Prep Ahead

Set each person's work area with a character template, and set out enough markers, crayons, yarn, scissors, googly eyes, and glue. Set out your premade character for everyone to see.

Notes

Character Creation works well with children who have challenging behaviors, as the focus is on their character, as opposed to themselves. They can assign character traits to their character that they may be striving to achieve on their own.

Activity Reminder

Include the Creative Outlet Method components throughout the activity.

1. HIPPP Rules.
2. A+ Audience: "A+ back to spots by 3, A+ back to spots by 2, A+ back to spots by 1. Great job! I really like how [say the name of the person] is sitting A+. I also like how [say the name of the person] is sitting A+."
3. "I like how [say the name of the person] is showing [say the component of the HIPPP Rules that the person is exhibiting]."
4. "Hey, Hey What?!"
5. The Ferris Wheel Round of Applause.

Facilitator Activity

Welcome: 1 minute

1. Welcome everyone and share how excited you are for your child and peers and/or family members to create and perform their own unique character.

Create Character: 10 minutes

2. Let your child and guests know that they can start to create their character. Show them your pre-made character.

3. Tell them your character's traits:

   Name

   Age

   Favorite food

   Where they are from

   Their favorite activity

4. Use a different voice to portray how your character sounds. Move around like your character.

5. Ask them to think of those character traits as they create their character.

Rehearsal: 4–5 minutes

6. Let everyone know that they will rehearse their character performance.

7. Have each participant share their character's traits:

   Name

   Age

   Favorite food

   Where they are from

   Their favorite activity

8. Have each participant perform as their character by using their character's voice and moving like their character.

Intro: 1 minute

9. Announce, "Ladies and gentlemen, I am excited to have these great folks share their characters with you. And away we go!"

Performance: 4–5 minutes

10. Have each participant share their character's traits:

    Name

    Age

    Favorite food

    Where they are from

    Their favorite activity

11. Have each participant perform as their character by using their character's voice and moving like their character.

Performance Conclusion: 3 minutes

12. Gesture for the performers to stand in a line facing the audience. Lead the performers in taking a bow.

Your Child's Activity

Welcome: 1 minute

1. Your child, along with peers and/or family members, stands with you.

Create Character: 10 minutes

2. Your child, along with peers and/or family members, begins to work on their character using the arts and crafts supplied.

Rehearsal: 4–5 minutes

3. Your child shares their character going through each character trait.

4. Your child performs as their character as they portray the character's voice and movements.

Intro: 1 minute

5. Your child's peers and/or family members are arranged sitting or standing to face the audience.

Performance: 4–5 minutes

6. Your child shares their character going through each character trait.

7. Your child performs as their character as they portray the character's voice and movements.

Performance Conclusion: 1 minute

8. Your child and peers and/or family members bow for the audience.

Visual Cues

Character templates printed on cardstock

Premade character made on card stock

Expected Outcomes

Welcome

1. Your child feels comfortable, excited, patient, and confident while waiting to create their character.

Create Character

2. Your child creates and illustrates their character with little to no prompting from you.

Rehearsal

3. Your child rehearses as their character.

Intro

4. Your child feels comfortable, excited, patient, and confident while waiting to perform.

Performance

5. Your child performs as their character.

Performance Conclusion

6. Your child increases self-confidence while performing for an audience.

Hey, Hey What?!

Goal

To demonstrate their creativity by performing in various scenes.

Objectives

1. Create settings that can be followed by others.
2. Increase self-confidence while performing the role of the group leader.
3. Build social skills by taking turns and following a leader.

Materials

Character card

Prep Ahead

Have the person playing Toast wear the character card.

Notes

Hey, Hey What?! is a common theater arts game. In my version, Toast performs as the leader – in theater we call this the Director. This game inspired the Hey, Hey What?! of my HIPPP Rules.

Activity Reminder

Include the Creative Outlet Method components throughout the activity.

1. HIPPP Rules.
2. A+ Audience: "A+ back to spots by 3, A+ back to spots by 2, A+ back to spots by 1. Great job! I really like how [say the name of the person] is sitting A+. I also like how [say the name of the person] is sitting A+."
3. "I like how [say the name of the person] is showing [say the component of the HIPPP Rules that the person is exhibiting]."
4. "Hey, Hey What?!"
5. The Ferris Wheel Round of Applause.

Facilitator Activity

Welcome: 1 minute

1. Welcome everyone and share how excited you are for your child and peers and/or family members to play a game together.

Part 1: 1 minute

2. Explain to everyone that the leader will perform as Toast, and that everyone will have a chance to be the leader.
3. Have your child play the role of Toast first.

Part 2: 1 minute

4. Everyone stands in the designated performance space while Toast loudly says, "Hey!"

5. The other participants respond by saying, "Hey, what?!"

Part 3: 1 minute

6. Toast tells everyone the setting of the scene by saying, "Hey, let's all go to the [Toast says the setting, such as: the movies, the jungle, the desert, the video game place, a BBQ restaurant, the airport, the zoo, etc.]. Everyone performs like they are in the setting that Toast described. For example, if Toast said, "Hey, let's all go to the jungle," then everyone would pretend to be walking through tall plants and looking at jungle animals.

Part 4: 1 minute

7. After about a minute of the group performing, you can conclude the round and have everyone applaud for each other.

8. Ask who would like to perform as Toast for the next round and provide that person with the character card.

Your Child's Activity

Welcome: 1 minute

9. Your child, along with peers and/or family members, stands with you.

Part 1: 1 minute

10. Your child, along with peers and/or family members, stands with you.

Part 2: 1 minute

11. Toast tells everyone the setting of the scene by saying, "Hey, let's all go to the [Toast says the setting, such as: the movies, the jungle, the desert, the video game place, a BBQ restaurant, the airport, the zoo, etc.].

Part 3: 1 minute

12. Your child and peers perform.

Part 4: 1 minute

13. Your child gives you the character card.

Visual Cues

Character card

Expected Outcomes

Welcome and Part 1

1. Your child feels comfortable, excited, patient, and confident while waiting to play the game.

Parts 2 and 3

2. Your child creates a setting that the others in the group could follow.

3. Your child feels confident while performing in the role of the group leader.

Part 4

4. Your child's social skills increase while playing the role of both leader and follower.

Object Transformations

Goal

To demonstrate creativity using common household objects.

Objectives

1. Demonstrate creativity by pretending a given object is used for something entirely different than its intended purpose.

2. Increase self-confidence by performing an object's alternative use in front of peers.

3. Build social skills by taking turns.

Materials

Wooden spoon

Banana

Towel

Pen/pencil

Bucket/pail

Hat

Shirt

Stuffed animal

Shoe

Book

Pillow

Any other age-appropriate objects

Prep Ahead

Gather enough objects so there are at least 3 to 4 objects per person.

Notes

In this activity, a banana can be a phone or even a writing implement. You get the idea.

Activity Reminder

Include the Creative Outlet Method components throughout the activity.

1. HIPPP Rules.

2. A+ Audience: "A+ back to spots by 3, A+ back to spots by 2, A+ back to spots by 1. Great job! I really like how [say the name of the person] is sitting A+. I also like how [say the name of the person] is sitting A+."

3. "I like how [say the name of the person] is showing [say the component of the HIPPP Rules that the person is exhibiting]."

4. "Hey, Hey What?!"

5. The Ferris Wheel Round of Applause.

Facilitator Activity

Welcome: 1 minute

1. Welcome everyone and share how excited you are for their child and peers and/or family members to play the game with everyone.

2. Have everyone join you in a circle. Announce, "Today we are going to take objects from the center of our circle and magically turn them into something else. Like this."

3. Pick up one of the objects, such as a wooden spoon, and show the object to everyone. Ask, "What is this?"

4. They should respond that the object is a spoon. Say, "That's right. Normally it would be a wooden spoon. Today this is a microphone."

5. Talk or sing into the wooden spoon as if it were a microphone.

6. "Okay, who's ready to take an object and make it something else?"

Objects: 5 minutes

7. Have your child select an object. Then encourage your child to come up with a different use for the object.

8. Continue for all the participants until everyone has 3 to 4 objects.

Conclusion: 1 minute

9. Conclude by saying, "Thank you, everyone, for creating new uses for these objects. Great job!"

10. Gesture for the performers to stand in a line facing the audience. Lead the performers in taking a bow.

Your Child's Activity

Welcome: 1 minute

1. Your child, along with peers and/or family members, stands with you.

Example: 1 minute

2. Your child watches you explain and demonstrate the activity.

Objects: 5 minutes

3. Your child selects objects and pretends they are used for something other than their intended use.

Conclusion: 1 minute

4. Your child and peers and/or family members bow for the audience.

Visual Cues

Objects

Expected Outcomes

Welcome

1. Your child feels comfortable, excited, patient, and confident while waiting to play the game.

Example

2. Your child feels comfortable, excited, patient, and confident while waiting to play the game.

Objects

3. Your child demonstrates creativity by pretending a given object is used for something entirely different from its intended purpose.

4. Your child increases self-confidence by performing an object's alternative use in front of peers.

5. Your child builds social skills by taking turns with peers.

Conclusion

6. Your child increases self-confidence while performing for an audience.

Comic Strip

Goal

To create and share their own comic strip.

Objectives

1. Create at least two characters.
2. Create a plot including a beginning, a middle, and an end.
3. Increase self-confidence by presenting the comic strip to an audience.

Materials

Comic strip template

Colored pencils

Regular pencils

Black, fine-tip markers

Premade comic strip

Prep Ahead

Print enough Comic Strip templates for each participant. Make your own comic strip prior to the activity. You can support non-readers and non-writers by allowing them to only draw their comic strip illustrations.

Notes

Comic Strip is a common activity that fosters creativity. In my version I have the participants use voices for their comic strip characters.

Activity Reminder

Include the Creative Outlet Method components throughout the activity.

1. HIPPP Rules.
2. A+ Audience: "A+ back to spots by 3, A+ back to spots by 2, A+ back to spots by 1. Great job! I really like how [say the name of the person] is sitting A+. I also like how [say the name of the person] is sitting A+."
3. "I like how [say the name of the person] is showing [say the component of the HIPPP Rules that the person is exhibiting]."
4. "Hey, Hey What?!"
5. The Ferris Wheel Round of Applause.

Facilitator Activity

Welcome: 1 minute

1. Welcome everyone and share how excited you are for your child and peers and/or family members to create and share their own unique comic strip.

Create Comic Strip: 30 minutes

2. Let your child and guests know that they can start to create their comic strip. Show them your premade comic strip.
3. Share your comic strip by using different voices for each character.

4. Ask them to think of different characters as they begin to create their comic strips.

Rehearsal: 10 minutes

5. Let everyone know that they will rehearse sharing their comic strip.

6. Have each participant share their comic strip. Encourage everyone to use different voices for the characters.

Intro: 1 minute

7. Announce, "Ladies and gentlemen, I am excited to have these great folks share their comic strips with you. And away we go!"

Performance: 10 minutes

8. Have each participant share their comic strip. Encourage everyone to use different voices for the characters.

Performance Conclusion: 1 minute

9. Gesture for the performers to stand in a line facing the audience. Lead the performers in taking a bow.

Your Child's Activity

Welcome: 1 minute

1. Your child, along with peers and/or family members, stands with you.

Create Comic Strip: 30 minutes

2. Your child, along with peers and/or family members, begins to work on their comic strip using the materials supplied by you.

Rehearsal: 10 minutes

3. Your child shares their comic strip as they portray the characters' voices.

Intro: 1 minute

4. Your child's peers and/or family members are arranged sitting or standing to face the audience.

Performance: 10 minutes

5. Your child shares their comic strip as they portray the characters' voices.

Performance Conclusion: 1 minute

6. Your child and peers and/or family members bow for the audience.

Visual Cues

Welcome and Create Comic Strip

1. Premade comic strip

Rehearsal, Intro, Performance, and Performance Conclusion

2. Comic strips

Expected Outcomes

Welcome

1. Your child feels comfortable, excited, patient, and confident while waiting to create their character.

Create Comic Strip

2. Your child creates at least 2 characters.

3. Your child creates a plot including a beginning, a middle, and an end.

Rehearsal

4. Your child presents their comic strip to peers.

Intro

5. Your child feels comfortable, excited, patient, and confident while waiting to perform.

Performance

6. Your child presents their comic strip to the audience.

Performance Conclusion

7. Your child increases self-confidence while performing for an audience.

Categories

Goal

To think quickly while participating in a game.

Objectives

1. Follow the rules of the game at least 8 out of 12 times.

2. Demonstrate creativity by thinking quickly at least 8 out of 12 times.

3. Demonstrate social skills by waiting for a turn during a complete round of the game at least 6 out of 8 times.

Prep Ahead

Think of groups that easily include specific types, such as: colors, cars, superheroes, vegetables, animals, cereal, video games, and movies.

Notes

Categories is a popular improvisational game frequently played at camps and theater programs. Your child and the other children may feel discouraged when they are eliminated from a round. You can support them by reminding them that they will select the next category of the next round.

Activity Reminder

Include the Creative Outlet Method components throughout the activity.

1. HIPPP Rules.

2. A+ Audience: "A+ back to spots by 3, A+ back to spots by 2, A+ back to spots by 1. Great job! I really like how [say the name of the person] is sitting A+. I also like how [say the name of the person] is sitting A+."

3. "I like how [say the name of the person] is showing [say the component of the HIPPP Rules that the person is exhibiting]."

4. "Hey, Hey What?!"

5. The Ferris Wheel Round of Applause.

Facilitator Activity

Welcome: 1 minute

1. Welcome everyone and share how excited you are for your child and peers and/or family members to perform for everyone.

Intro: 2 minutes

2. Share with everyone how the game is played:

3. "Line up single file in the performance area facing the audience."

4. "At the start of each round I'll name a category, such as types of cars. Then I'll point to each of you one at a time, and you have 5 seconds to say a type of car, such as a race car, sports car, sedan, and so on. You can also name car companies if you like."

5. "If you don't have a type at the end of the 5 seconds, or if you say something other than a type of car, or if you say a type that has already been said, you are out of the round."

6. "Being out means you join me in the audience, and you get to pick the next category."

7. "The last person standing is the winner."

Round 1: 2–3 minutes

8. Begin the round by letting everyone know you are starting the round.

9. As the game begins, encourage everyone to do a great job.

Round 2: 2–3 minutes

10. Ask the player who was out in round 1 to select the next category. You can give suggestions as needed.

11. Begin the round by letting everyone know you are starting the round.

12. As the game begins, encourage everyone to do a great job.

Round 3: 2–3 minutes

13. Ask the player who was out in round 2 to select the next category. You can give suggestions as needed.

14. Begin the round by letting everyone know you are starting the round.

15. As the game begins, encourage everyone to do a great job.

Round 4: 2–3 minutes

16. Ask the player who was out in round 3 to select the next category. You can give suggestions as needed.

17. Begin the round by letting everyone know you are starting the round.

18. As the game begins, encourage everyone to do a great job.

19. Continue into round 5 if desired or thank everyone for playing and having fun.

Your Child's Activity

Welcome: 1 minute

1. Your child, along with peers and/or family members, stands with you.

Intro: 2 minutes

2. Your child, along with peers and/or family members, listens to how the game is played.

Round 1: 2–3 minutes

3. Your child and peers and/or family members engage in the game.

4. Each player says a type within the category on cue, or a player leaves the round if they are unable to think of a type in 5 seconds, or if they repeat a type that was already said.

Rounds 2 to 4: 2–3 minutes each

5. Each player says a type within the category on cue, or a player leaves the round if they are unable to think of a type in 5 seconds, or if they repeat a type that was already said.

Expected Outcomes

Welcome

1. Your child feels comfortable, excited, patient, and confident while waiting to perform.

Intro

2. Your child feels comfortable, excited, patient, and confident while waiting to play the game.

Rounds 1–4

3. Your child follows the rules of the game at least 2 out of 3 times.

4. Your child thinks of a type at least 2 out of 3 times.

5. Your child waits for their turn at least 2 out of 3 times.

Statues in the Park

Goal

To demonstrate their creativity by performing as a statue or a guard during a game.

Objectives

1. Demonstrate creativity by performing as a statue posing in various positions, or by performing as a guard.

2. Increase self-confidence by performing as the guard.

3. Build social skills by following the rules of the game.

Notes

Statues in the Park is a popular game played in many programs. Participants may claim that they weren't moving when they are told to melt. I recommend permitting the participants to resolve the conflict on their own, and to intervene only if the behavior becomes a pattern.

Activity Reminder

Include the Creative Outlet Method components throughout the activity.

1. HIPPP Rules.

2. A+ Audience: "A+ back to spots by 3, A+ back to spots by 2, A+ back to spots by 1. Great job! I really like how [say the name of the person] is sitting A+. I also like how [say the name of the person] is sitting A+."

3. "I like how [say the name of the person] is showing [say the component of the HIPPP Rules that the person is exhibiting]."

4. "Hey, Hey What?!"

5. The Ferris Wheel Round of Applause.

Facilitator Activity

Welcome: 1 minute

1. Welcome everyone and share how excited you are for your child and peers and/or family members to play a game together.

Intro part 1: 1 minute

2. Have everyone sit in a circle.

3. Announce, "I have some great news. We are about to travel far away from here. We are about to go to a park, a magical park, with moving statues! Who's ready to come with me?"

4. Continue, "Everyone will get to be a magic statue, and one person will be the guard looking for moving statues. The guard's job is to look for statues that are moving. If the guard sees a statue move, the guard will point to the moving statue and the guard will tell that statue to melt. Statues need to fall to the ground if told to melt.

Statues will want to move around when the guard isn't looking."

5. Ask, "Who wants to be the first guard?"

6. Select your child to be the guard.

7. Continue, "Great! Everyone else is a statue. Statues, spread out across our magical park and get into a statue position. Don't let the guard catch you moving."

8. Continue, "Statues in statue position by 3 . . . statues in statue position by 2 . . . statues in statue position by 1, and hold it there."

9. Continue, "Okay, time for the guard to start looking for moving statues. Good luck!"

Round 1: 3 minutes

10. Help the guard move around looking for statues that are moving. If the guard sees a statue move, the guard points to that statue and tells him/her to melt.

11. Help the statues as needed to melt when they are told to melt.

12. When 2 statues are left standing, announce that they are the winners of the round.

13. Have everyone applaud for each other.

14. Ask who would like to be the next guard.

Round 2 and more: 12 minutes total

15. Follow the steps from above until everyone has an opportunity to be the guard.

Conclusion: 1 minute

16. Gesture for the performers to stand in a line facing the audience. Lead the performers in taking a bow.

Your Child's Activity

Welcome: 1 minute

1. Your child, along with peers and/or family members, stands with you.

Intro, Parts 1 and 2: 1 minute each

2. Your child, along with peers, listens to you provide instructions for the activity.

Round 1: 3 minutes

3. Your child moves around and between the statues looking for movement.

4. Your child points to a moving statue and says "melt" to the moving statues.

Round 2 and more:
12 minutes total

5. Your child poses in various positions as a statue when the guard isn't looking.

6. Your child melts to the ground when the guard tells him/her to melt for moving.

Conclusion: 1 minute

7. Your child and peers and/or family members bow for the audience.

Expected Outcomes

Welcome, Intro part 1, and Intro part 2

1. Your child feels comfortable, excited, patient, and confident while waiting to perform.

Round 1

2. Your child demonstrates creativity by performing as the guard.

3. Your child increases self-confidence by performing as the guard.

4. Your child builds social skills by following the rules of the game.

Round 2 and more

5. Your child demonstrates creativity by performing as a statue posing in various positions.

6. Your child builds social skills by following the rules of the game.

Conclusion

7. Your child increases self-confidence while performing for an audience.

Juice

Goal

To demonstrate creativity while playing an imaginative game.

Objectives

1. Demonstrate creativity while pretending to hold an object.

2. Increase self-confidence by performing with the group.

3. Build social skills by following a leader.

Notes

Juice is an activity I created. I like this activity because it's like a dance where all of us are performing the same movements at the same time for the duration of the activity. The faster you move through the "hands on head" routine, the more the participants will be engaged. Sometimes I can see our imaginary cups of juice magically appear, and I am sure yours will, too.

Activity Reminder

Include the Creative Outlet Method components throughout the activity.

1. HIPPP Rules.

2. A+ Audience: "A+ back to spots by 3, A+ back to spots by 2, A+ back to spots by 1. Great job! I really like how [say the name of the person] is sitting A+. I also like how [say the name of the person] is sitting A+."

3. "I like how [say the name of the person] is showing [say the component of the HIPPP Rules that the person is exhibiting]."

4. "Hey, Hey What?!"

5. The Ferris Wheel Round of Applause.

Facilitator Activity

Welcome: 1 minute

1. Welcome everyone and share how excited you are for your child and peers and/or family members to play the game with everyone.

Intro: Cup: 1 minute

2. Have everyone join you in a circle on the floor. Make sure everyone is sitting cross-legged.

3. You say, "Is anybody thirsty? We are about to make our very own juice.

4. "To make sure you're ready, I want you to do what I do: hands on head [put your hands on your head so everyone will follow], hands on knees [put your hands on your knees so everyone will follow], hands on shoulders [put your hands on your shoulders so everyone will follow], and hands out

[extend your arms to your left and right and so everyone will follow]. Hold your hands there while I give each of you your own cup."

5. Pretend you are putting an empty cup in each person's hands.

Apple: 1 minute

6. Continue by saying, "I want to make sure everyone is ready for the first ingredient. Hands on head, hands on knees, hands on shoulders, and hands out."

7. Pretend that you are taking an apple out of the sky.

8. Continue by saying, "Great. You are ready for the first ingredient. Everyone gets an apple."

9. Pretend that you are putting an apple in everyone's hands.

10. Continue by saying, "Now take that apple, and hold it up."

11. Pretend you are holding an apple at eye level, and make sure everyone else is doing it.

12. Say, "Now take that apple and mush it, and smush it, and make all that apple juice fall into your cup."

13. Pretend you are mushing and smushing an apple and getting the juice to fall into your imaginary cup, and make sure everyone else is doing it.

14. Continue by saying, "Now wipe off the apple chunks from your lap."

15. Pretend that you are wiping large apple chunks from your lap, and make sure everyone else is doing it.

16. "Wipe them off your shoulders."

17. Pretend you are wiping large apple chunks off your shoulders, and make sure everyone else is doing it.

18. "Wipe them off your hair." Pretend you are wiping large apple chunks off your hair, and make sure everyone else is doing it. "Throw the rest of the apple chunks every-where." Pretend you are throwing large apple chunks all over the place, and make sure everyone else is doing it.

First Juice Sniff: 1 minute

19. Continue by saying, "Now pick up your cup of juice."

20. Make an exaggerated movement while pretending to pick up your imaginary cup of juice, raising it to eye level, and make sure everyone else is doing it.

21. "Swirl it around."

22. Pretend you are swirling around your cup of juice and make sure everyone else is doing it.

23. "Smell it."

24. Pretend you are smelling your cup of juice, and make sure everyone else is doing it.

25. "And put it back down."

26. Pretend you are putting your cup on the floor, and make sure everyone else is doing it, too.

Broccoli: 1 minute

27. Continue by saying, "Hands on head, hands on knees, hands on shoulders, and hands out."

28. Pretend you are taking broccoli out of the sky.

29. Continue by saying, "Great. You are ready for the next ingredient. Everyone gets 5-year-old, rotten broccoli."

30. Pretend you are putting broccoli in everyone's hands.

31. Continue by saying, "Now take that broccoli, and hold it up."

32. Pretend you are holding broccoli at eye level, and make sure everyone else is doing it.

33. "Now take that broccoli and mush it, and smush it, and make all that rotten, smelly juice fall into your cup."

34. Pretend you are mushing and smushing the broccoli and getting the juice to fall into your imaginary cup, and make sure everyone else is doing it.

35. Continue by saying, "Now wipe off the rotten smelly broccoli mush on your lap."

36. Pretend you are wiping mushy broccoli from your lap, and make sure everyone else is doing it.

37. "Wipe it off your shoulders."

38. Pretend you are wiping mushy broccoli off your shoulders, and make sure everyone else is doing it.

39. "Wipe it off your hair."

40. Pretend you are wiping mushy broccoli from your hair, and make sure everyone else is doing it.

41. "Throw the rest of the mushy broccoli everywhere."

42. Pretend you are throwing mushy broccoli all over the place, and make sure everyone else is doing it.

Second Juice Sniff: 1 minute

43. Continue by saying, "Now pick up your cup of juice."

44. Make an exaggerated movement while pretending to pick up your imaginary cup of juice, raising it to eye level, and make sure everyone else is doing it.

45. "Swirl it around."

46. Pretend you are swirling around your cup of juice, and make sure everyone else is doing it.

47. "Smell it and say pee-yew-peek-a-choo."

48. Pretend that you are smelling your cup of juice, and make sure everyone else is doing it. Lead everyone in saying, "pee-yew-peek-a-choo" and wave your hand back and forth in front of your nose.

49. "And put it back down."

50. Pretend you are putting your cup on the floor and make sure everyone else is doing it, too.

Dirty Socks: 1 minute

51. "Hands on head, hands on knees, hands on shoulders, and hands out."

52. Pretend you are taking dirty socks out of the sky.

53. Continue by saying, "Great. You are ready for the next ingredient. Everyone gets dirty socks."

54. Pretend you are putting dirty socks in everyone's hands.

55. Continue by saying, "Now take those dirty socks, and hold them up."

56. Pretend you are holding the dirty socks at eye level, and make sure everyone else is doing it.

57. "Now take those dirty socks and move them all around until they make dirty sock juice fall into your cup."

58. Pretend you are twirling dirty socks around and getting the juice to fall into your imaginary cup, and make sure everyone else is doing it.

59. Continue by saying, "Now wipe off the dirty sock stinky smell from your lap."

60. Pretend you are wiping dirty sock stinky smell from your lap, and make sure everyone else is doing it.

61. "Wipe it off your shoulders."

62. Pretend you are wiping the dirty sock stinky smell off your shoulders, and make sure everyone else is doing it.

63. "Wipe it off your hair."

64. Pretend you are wiping dirty sock stinky smell off your hair, and make sure everyone else is doing it.

65. "Throw the rest of the dirty sock stinky smell everywhere."

66. Pretend you are throwing dirty sock stinky smell all over the place, and make sure everyone else is doing it.

Juice Sniff 3: 1 minute

67. "Now pick up your cup of juice."

68. Make an exaggerated movement while pretending to pick up your imaginary cup of juice, raising it to eye level, and make sure everyone else is doing it.

69. "Swirl it around."

70. Pretend you are swirling around your cup of juice and make sure everyone else is doing it.

71. "Smell it and say pee-yew-peek-a-choo."

72. Pretend you are smelling your cup of juice, and make sure everyone else is doing it. Lead everyone in saying, "pee-yew-peek-a-choo" and wave your hand back and forth in front of your nose.

73. "And put it back down."

74. Pretend you are putting your cup on the floor and make sure everyone else is doing it, too.

Pour the Juice: 1 minute

75. "Now pick up your cup of juice."

76. Bring your cup of juice to eye level and make sure everybody else is doing it.

77. "Smell that juice with apple, mushy 5-year-old rotten broccoli, and dirty socks."

78. Smell the juice and make sure everyone else is doing it.

79. "Put that cup of juice near the person sitting next to you. Put it right by their ear."

80. Put your juice next to a person's ear.

81. "Now take that juice and dump it on that person's head!"

82. Dump your juice on the person's head.

Conclusion: 1 minute

83. "Thank you everyone for making amazing juice with me today. Great job!"

84. Gesture for the performers to stand in a line facing the audience. Lead the performers in taking a bow.

Your Child's Activity

Welcome: 1 minute

1. Your child, along with peers and/or family members, stands with you.

Intro: Cup: 1 minute

2. Your child follows your lead and places hands on head, knees, and shoulders.

3. Your child puts out hands to wait for the imaginary juice cup.

Apple: 1 minute

4. Your child follows your lead and places hands on head, knees, and shoulders.

5. Your child puts out hands to wait for the ingredient.

6. Your child follows your lead and mushes and smushes an apple to make the juice.

7. Your child follows your lead and wipes imaginary apple chunks from lap, shoulders, and hair, then pretends to throw chunks all around.

First Juice Sniff: 1 minute

8. Your child follows your lead to sniff the cup of juice.

Broccoli: 1 minute

9. Your child follows your lead and places their hands on head, knees, and shoulders.

10. Your child puts out hands to wait for the ingredient.

11. Your child follows your lead and mushes and smushes the broccoli to make the juice.

12. Your child follows your lead and wipes off rotten smelly broccoli mush.

Second Juice Sniff: 1 minute

13. Your child follows your lead to sniff the cup of juice.

Dirty Socks: 1 minute

14. Your child follows your lead and places hands on head, knees, and shoulders.

15. Your child puts out hands to wait for the ingredient.

16. Your child takes the dirty socks and pretends to twirl them around.

17. Your child follows your lead and twirls the dirty socks to make the juice.

18. Your child follows your lead and wipes off the dirty sock smell.

Juice Sniff 3: 1 minute

19. Your child follows your lead to sniff the cup of juice.

Pour the Juice: 1 minute

20. Your child follows your lead to pour the cup of juice on someone.

Conclusion: 1 minute

21. Your child and peers and/or family members bow for the audience.

Expected Outcomes

Welcome

1. Your child feels comfortable, excited, patient, and confident while waiting to play the game.

Intro: Cup, Apple, and First Juice Sniff

2. Your child builds social skills by following the leader's movements.

3. Your child demonstrates creativity by pretending to hold an empty cup.

4. Your child increases self-confidence by performing the activity with peers and/or family members.

5. Your child demonstrates creativity by pretending to hold an apple, make apple juice, wipe off and throw apple chunks, and smell a cup of juice.

Broccoli and Second Juice Sniff

6. Your child builds social skills by following the leader's movements.

7. Your child demonstrates creativity by pretending to hold broccoli.

8. Your child increases self-confidence by performing the activity with peers and/or family members.

9. Your child demonstrates creativity by pretending to make broccoli juice, wipe off rotten smelly broccoli mush, and smell a cup of juice.

Dirty Socks and Third Juice Sniff

10. Your child builds social skills by following the leader's movements.

11. Your child increases self-confidence by performing the activity with peers and/or family members.

12. Your child demonstrates creativity by pretending to hold dirty socks, making juice out of dirty socks. wipe off the dirty sock smell, and smell a cup of juice.

Pour the Juice

13. Your child demonstrates creativity by pretending to pour out a cup of juice.

Conclusion

14. Your child increases self-confidence as they perform for an audience.

Pizza

Goal

To demonstrate creativity while playing an imaginative game.

Objectives

1. Demonstrate creativity while pretending to hold an object.
2. Increase self-confidence by performing with the group.
3. Build social skills by following a leader.

Prep Ahead

Learn the dance steps ahead of time so you can confidently move through the activity.

Notes

Pizza is one of my own activities, and there is so much fun to be had. Adults enjoy Pizza as well. I typically save this one for the end of a workshop, or just before we do Create a Story.

Activity Reminder

Include the Creative Outlet Method components throughout the activity.

1. HIPPP Rules.
2. A+ Audience: "A+ back to spots by 3, A+ back to spots by 2, A+ back to spots by 1. Great job! I really like how [say the name of the person] is sitting A+. I also like how [say the name of the person] is sitting A+."
3. "I like how [say the name of the person] is showing [say the component of the HIPPP Rules that the person is exhibiting]."
4. "Hey, Hey What?!"
5. The Ferris Wheel Round of Applause.

Facilitator Activity

Welcome: 1 minute

1. Welcome everyone and share how excited you are for your child and peers and/or family members to play the game with everyone.

Intro: 1 minute

2. Have everyone stand in a circle. Announce, "Who is feeling hungry? Who is ready for a snack? We are going to make our own snack, right here, right now. We are going to make a pizza!"

Dough: 1 minute

3. Announce, "To start making our pizza, we need to make the dough. I need two volunteers to be the dough."
4. After you have the volunteers, have them sit on the floor facing each other.
5. Continue, "Great. You two are the dough. You need rolling pins to

roll out the dough. Roll the dough while saying '*dough, dough, dough.*' Ready, set, go! '*Dough, dough, dough, dough, dough.*'"

6. Rolling the dough: Pretend to hold a rolling pin and roll the dough to the front and back quickly as you say "*dough.*"

Sauce: 1 minute

7. Tell everyone that you need 2 volunteers for the next part of making the pizza, which is the sauce.

8. Have the sauce volunteers stand over the dough volunteers. Teach the sauce volunteers the sauce dance.

9. Sauce dance: Move your hips side-to-side while holding your hands flat, palms down, moving them in the opposite direction of your hips, while you say "su-su-sauce-su-su-sauce- su-su-sauce."

10. Once the sauce volunteers have the sauce dance underway, have the dough volunteers roll their dough.

11. Let the scene continue for about 20 seconds.

Cheese: 1 minute

12. Tell everyone, "Hold it. Freeze. Pause. Hold scene. We can't just have a saucy pizza today. Who's feeling cheesy? We need 2 cheesy people to be the cheese."

13. Once you have 2 volunteers, teach them the cheese dance.

14. Cheese dance: Bring your arms up straight above your head, wiggle your fingers as you lower your arms and raise them again, while saying "ch-ch-ch-cheese, ch-ch-ch-cheese, ch- ch-ch-ch-cheese."

15. Once the cheese volunteers have the cheese dance underway, have the sauce volunteers start the sauce dance, and then bring in the dough volunteers.

16. Let the scene continue for about 20 seconds.

Pepperoni: 1 minute

17. Tell everyone, "Hold it. Freeze. Pause. Hold scene. We can't just make a cheese pizza today. We have customers in my restaurant who love pepperoni. Two volunteers are needed to be our pepperoni today."

18. Once you have 2 volunteers, teach them the pepperoni dance.

19. Pepperoni dance: Move your arms to the left of your body and shake them twice, then move your arms to the right of your body and shake them twice, while saying "pep-pep-er-oni, pep-pep-er-oni, pep-pep-er-oni."

20. Once the pepperoni volunteers have the pepperoni dance under way, have the cheese volunteers

start the cheese dance, then the sauce volunteers start the sauce dance, and then bring in the dough volunteers.

21. Let the scene continue for about 20 seconds.

Dirty Socks: 1 minute

22. Tell everyone, "Hold it. Freeze. Pause. Hold scene. We need one more ingredient for this pizza. Oh, my goodness, this will be the best ingredient, ever. Who would like to be dirty socks? Yes, that's right, dirty socks."

23. Once you have two volunteers, teach them the dirty socks dance.

24. Dirty socks dance: Hold up your right arm and pretend to twirl around a pair of socks, then pretend to wave them in front of your face, throw them over your shoulder, and say "pee-yew-peek-a-choo."

25. Once the dirty socks volunteers have the dirty socks dance underway, have the pepperoni volunteers do the pepperoni dance, the cheese volunteers do the cheese dance, the sauce volunteers start the sauce dance, and then bring in the dough volunteers.

26. Let the scene continue for about 20 seconds.

Crust: 1 minute

27. Tell everyone, "Hold it. Freeze. Pause. Hold scene. We're almost done with the pizza. We need the last, final part. Anybody know what the final part is? It's the crust. Let's have everyone else be the crust."

28. Teach the rest of the group the crust dance.

29. Crust dance: Walk in a circle around the other volunteers, moving your head back and forth in big dramatic movements while saying "cruh-uh-uh-st, cruh-uh-uh-st."

30. Once the crust volunteers have the crust dance underway, have the dirty socks volunteers start their dance, have the pepperoni volunteers do the pepperoni dance, the cheese volunteers do the cheese dance, the sauce volunteers start the sauce dance, and then bring in the dough volunteers.

31. Let the scene continue for about 20 seconds.

Conclusion: 1 minute

32. Conclude by saying, "Thank you everyone for making a fabulous pizza with me today. Great job!"

33. Gesture for the performers to stand in a line facing the audience. Lead the performers in taking a bow.

Your Child's Activity

Welcome and Intro: 1 minute

1. Your child, along with peers and/or family members, stands with you.

Dough, Sauce, Cheese, Pepperoni, Dirty Socks, Crust: 1 minute

2. Your child volunteers or watches as the volunteers begin their role.

Conclusion: 1 minute

3. Your child and peers and/or family members bow for the audience.

Expected Outcomes

Welcome and Intro

1. Your child feels comfortable, excited, patient, and confident while waiting to play the game.

Dough, Sauce, Cheese, Pepperoni, Dirty Socks, and Crust

2. Your child demonstrates creativity by pretending to hold an object.

3. Your child increases self-confidence by performing with the group.

4. Your child builds social skills by following a leader.

Conclusion

5. Your child increases self-confidence while performing for an audience.

Mashed-Up Monologues

Goal

To demonstrate creativity by producing words and by performing a monologue.

Objectives

1. Demonstrate creativity by producing words that reflect the type of word being requested.

2. Increase self-confidence by performing a monologue using a character voice.

3. Build social skills by demonstrating patience as partners produce words.

Materials

Mashed-Up Monologues Worksheets

Pencils

Costumes (optional)

Various arts and crafts supplies, including markers, construction paper, scissors, glue, etc.

Prep Ahead

Create a Mashed-Up Monologues worksheet for each participant. Several Mashed-Up Monologues worksheets are available for you if you prefer not to make your own. Complete your own funny Mashed-Up Monologue worksheet prior to the activity and prepare to perform it as an example.

Notes

I love writing monologues for my participants, and I love watching their creativity unfold. After being inspired by *Mad Libs*, I combined both loves to create Mashed-Up Monologues. You can support non-readers by pairing them up with another participant who can serve as their buddy for prompting their lines, or you can prompt the lines.

Activity Reminder

Include the Creative Outlet Method components throughout the activity.

1. HIPPP Rules.

2. A+ Audience: "A+ back to spots by 3, A+ back to spots by 2, A+ back to spots by 1. Great job! I really like how [say the name of the person] is sitting A+. I also like how [say the name of the person] is sitting A+."

3. "I like how [say the name of the person] is showing [say the component of the HIPPP Rules that the person is exhibiting]."

4. "Hey, Hey What?!"

5. The Ferris Wheel Round of Applause.

Facilitator Activity

Intro: 2 minutes

1. Announce, "What in the world is a monologue? It's a long speech by one person. Today you are making your own funny monologue – a Mashed-Up Monologue! Kind of like this one."

2. Perform your Mashed-Up Monologue. The more fun you have with it, the more fun the participants will have as they create their own.

Setup: 1 minute

3. Announce, "To make your own Mashed-Up Monologues, everyone will work with a partner. I'll give each person a worksheet. The monologues are mashed-up because it is up to each of you to come up with words for your partner's monologue, as prompted by your partner."

4. Make sure everyone has a partner and that each pair has a place to work.

5. Give each person a Mashed-Up Monologue worksheet and a pencil.

6. Assign each person as Partner 1 or as Partner 2.

Partner 1: 2 minutes

7. Partner 1 will go through their Mashed-Up Monologue worksheet and ask Partner 2 for the words.

Partner 2: 2 minutes

8. When Partner 1 has completed their worksheet, Partner 2 will go through their Mashed-Up Monologue worksheet and ask Partner 1 for the words.

Monologue Practice: 5 minutes

9. When Partner 2 has completed their worksheet, have everyone read their monologues out loud, one at a time.

10. Let everyone know that they should figure out a fun way to perform their monologue, and everyone should practice their monologue for 5 minutes.

11. Help each person, as needed, figure out their monologues.

Performance: 5 minutes

12. When everyone is done practicing, announce, "Ladies and gentlemen, give a round of applause for our performers. We are about to watch these superstars perform their super-fun Mashed-Up Monologues. Let the show begin!"

13. Have each person perform their monologue.

Performance
Conclusion: 1 minute

14. Gesture for the performers to stand in a line facing the audience. Lead the performers in taking a bow.

Your Child's Activity

Intro: 1 minute

1. Your child, along with peers and/or family members, stands with you.

Setup: 1 minute

2. Your child finds a partner.

Partner 1: 2 minutes

3. Your child starts as Partner 1.

Partner 2: 2 minutes

4. Your child produces words for their partner's monologue.

Monologue Practice: 5 minutes

5. Your child practices monologue.

Performance: 5 minutes

6. Your child performs a monologue.

Performance
Conclusion: 1 minute

7. Your child and peers and/or family members bow for the audience.

Expected Outcomes

Intro

1. Your child feels comfortable, excited, patient, and confident while waiting to participate in the activity.

Setup

2. Your child, after finding a partner, feels comfortable, excited, patient, and confident while waiting to participate in the activity.

Partner 1

3. Your child builds social skills by demonstrating patience as their partner produces words.

Partner 2

4. Your child demonstrates creativity by producing words that reflect the type of word that is requested.

Monologue Practice and Performance

5. Your child increases self-confidence by performing a monologue using a character voice.

Performance Conclusion

6. Your child increases self-confidence while performing for an audience.

Monologues

Goal

To demonstrate creativity by producing words and by performing a monologue.

Objectives

1. Demonstrate creativity by performing as a character during a monologue.
2. Increase self-confidence by performing a monologue for an audience.
3. Build social skills by encouraging peers to perform successfully.

Materials

Monologues – the monologues can be found in the supplemental materials.

Prep Ahead

Prepare the monologues so that they are available for the participants.

Notes

You can support non-readers by pairing them up with another participant who can serve as their buddy for prompting their lines, or you can prompt the lines.

Activity Reminder

Include the Creative Outlet Method components throughout the activity.

1. HIPPP Rules.
2. A+ Audience: "A+ back to spots by 3, A+ back to spots by 2, A+ back to spots by 1. Great job! I really like how [say the name of the person] is sitting A+. I also like how [say the name of the person] is sitting A+."
3. "I like how [say the name of the person] is showing [say the component of the HIPPP Rules that the person is exhibiting]."
4. "Hey, Hey What?!"
5. The Ferris Wheel Round of Applause.

Facilitator Activity

Intro: 2 minutes

1. Announce, "What in the world is a monologue? It's a long speech by one person. Today you are performing your own monologue. Kind of like this one."
2. Perform your monologue. You can use the one I wrote called "Loom-Fa-Lilly-Poo-Grem," one you've written, or one you find online. The stronger your performance is, the better the participants will perform.

Monologue Assignments: 1 minute

3. Distribute the monologues from the supplemental materials to the participants, or you can write your own.

Monologue Read-Aloud: 5 minutes

4. Have everyone read their monologue out loud.

Monologue Practice: 20 minutes

5. Have everyone practice their monologues for about 20 minutes. You can help the participants as needed.

6. Have the participants face a wall while they practice their monologues. Facing the wall helps the performer let their character come alive.

Monologue Performances: 10 minutes

7. Have everyone perform their monologue.

Performance Conclusion: 1 minute

8. Gesture for the performers to stand in a line facing the audience.

9. Lead the performers in taking a bow.

Your Child's Activity

Intro: 2 minutes

1. Your child, along with peers and/or family members, stands with you.

2. Your child, along with peers, watches you perform your monologue.

Monologue Read-Aloud: 5 minutes

3. Your child reads aloud their monologue.

4. Your child encourages peers to read their monologues out loud.

Monologue Practice: 20 minutes

5. Your child reads aloud their monologue.

6. Your child encourages peers to read their monologues out loud.

7. Your child creates a character voice and mannerisms for the character in their monologue.

Monologue Performances: 10 minutes

8. Your child reads aloud their monologue.

9. Your child encourages peers to perform their monologues.

*Performance
Conclusion: 1 minute*

10. Your child and peers and/or family members bow for the audience.

Expected Outcomes

*Intro and Monologue
assignments*

1. Your child feels comfortable, excited, patient, and confident while waiting to participate in the activity.

Setup

2. Your child, after finding a partner, feels comfortable, excited, patient, and confident while waiting to participate in the activity.

*Monologue Read-Aloud, Practice,
and Performance*

3. Your child builds social skills by encouraging peers to read their monologue out loud.

4. Your child demonstrates creativity by performing as the character in their monologue.

5. Your child builds social skills by encouraging peers to perform well.

Performance Conclusion

6. Your child increases self-confidence while performing for an audience.

Yes, And

Goal

To perform using a specific prompt.

Objectives

1. Demonstrate creativity by creating a story using the prompt "Yes, and" before each part of the story.

2. Increase self-confidence by performing in front of an audience for the duration of the scene.

3. Build social skills by accepting and building on a peer's story ideas.

Materials

Yes, And character cards

Two chairs

Prep Ahead

Review my "Yes, and" example before you conduct the activity so you have an idea of how the scenes are conducted. Have the "Yes, and" character cards available. Set up two chairs in the designated performance space.

Notes

"Yes, and" is a popular game among improv programs because it promotes accepting and building upon the ideas of the people sharing the stage; a sense of trust is developed among the participants.

Activity Reminder

Include the Creative Outlet Method components throughout the activity.

1. HIPPP Rules.

2. A+ Audience: "A+ back to spots by 3, A+ back to spots by 2, A+ back to spots by 1. Great job! I really like how [say the name of the person] is sitting A+. I also like how [say the name of the person] is sitting A+."

3. "I like how [say the name of the person] is showing [say the component of the HIPPP Rules that the person is exhibiting]."

4. "Hey, Hey What?!"

5. The Ferris Wheel Round of Applause.

Facilitator Activity

Welcome: 1 minute

1. Welcome everyone and share how excited you are for your child and peers and/or family members to perform for everyone.

Intro: 1 minute

2. Have everyone sit in a circle. Announce, "We're going to play a game called Yes, And. We'll get a story going, and the 2 people telling the story have to say 'Yes, and' before the next part of the

story. We'll also have 2 performers acting out the story as it is told. We need 2 volunteers to be the storytellers, and 2 volunteers to be the performers."

3. Have your child as one of the storytellers. Have the storytellers sit in the chairs, and have the performers stand in front of the storytellers.

Round 1: 3 minutes

4. Ask the audience for story suggestions such as: the setting, how the performers are related, and the problem the performers are trying to solve.

5. Once the suggestions have been made, have your child be the first to start the story.

6. Have your child start the story with, "Yes, and . . ."

7. The performers act out what your child said.

8. Have the other storyteller create the next line of the story beginning with, "Yes, and . . ."

9. The scene ends when you decide it has gone on long enough.

Round 2 and Beyond: 3 minutes

10. Continue with as many rounds as needed so that each participant has an opportunity to be one of the storytellers or one of the performers.

Performance Conclusion: 1 minute

11. Gesture for the performers to stand in a line facing the audience.

12. Lead the performers in taking a bow.

Your Child's Activity

Welcome: 1 minute

1. Your child, along with peers and/or family members, stands with you.

Intro: 1 minute

2. Your child, along with peers and/or family members, sits in a circle with you.

3. Your child sits in one of the chairs for the storytellers.

Round 1: 3 minutes

4. Your child starts the story by using the prompt "Yes, and" relevant to the suggestions from the audience.

5. Your child listens and builds on the story ideas shared by their peers.

Round 2 and Beyond: 3 minutes

6. Your child performs according to the story prompts as told by the storytellers.

7. Your child and peers and/or family members bow for the audience.

Visual Cues

Character cards

Expected Outcomes

Welcome and Intro

1. Your child feels comfortable, excited, patient, and confident while waiting to perform.

Round 1, Round 2, Beyond, and Performance Conclusion

2. Your child demonstrates creativity by creating a story using the prompt "yes, and" before each part of the story.

3. Your child increases self-confidence by performing in front of an audience for the duration of the scene.

4. Your child builds social skills by accepting and building on a peer's story ideas.

Yes, And Example

The audience suggests that the story is taking place at a playground, the performers are brothers, and the problem they are trying to solve is who can slide down the slide in the coolest way.

Noah: "Yes, and I can slide down with my hands under my backside with my knees to my chest." (One of the performers gets down on the floor on their back and brings their knees to their chest while pretending to slide down a slide.)

Liam: "Yes, and I can slide down on my front side while holding my breath."

(One of the performers gets down on the floor on their front side and holds their breath while pretending to slide down a slide.)

Noah: "Yes, and I can go head first and spread my arms like I am flying at supersonic speed and sound like an airplane."

(One of the performers gets down on the floor, lies flat, and pretends to be flying down the slide head first while making airplane noises.)

Liam: "Yes, and I can slide down the slide while sitting up, chewing gum, patting my head, and rubbing my tummy."

(One of the performers sits on the floor, pretends to chew gum, pats their head, and rubs their tummy.)

The scene continues like this until you say the scene is over.

Alien Interview

Goal

To perform as a creature from another planet, a translator, and a game show host.

Objectives

1. Practice taking turns three out of three times.

2. Actively listen to peers.

3. Confidently perform as three characters.

Materials

Character cards

Three chairs

Microphone prop – examples include a wooden spoon, a whisk, a spatula

Solid-colored tape

Costumes (optional)

Prep Ahead

In your designated performance space, set up three chairs facing the audience. The performers wear their character cards. Provide the microphone prop to the person performing as Toast. Write Translator, Alien, and Toast separately on pieces of solid-colored tape and place each piece of tape on the top of a chair.

Notes

Alien Interview is a popular improvisational game frequently played at camps and theater programs. In my version, Toast is the host. You, your child, and their friends are encouraged to take turns performing each character.

Activity Reminder

Include the Creative Outlet Method components throughout the activity.

1. HIPPP Rules.

2. A+ Audience: "A+ back to spots by 3, A+ back to spots by 2, A+ back to spots by 1. Great job! I really like how [say the name of the person] is sitting A+. I also like how [say the name of the person] is sitting A+."

3. "I like how [say the name of the person] is showing [say the component of the HIPPP Rules that the person is exhibiting]."

4. "Hey, Hey What?!"

5. The Ferris Wheel Round of Applause.

Facilitator Activity

Welcome: 1 minute

1. Welcome everyone and share how excited you are for your child and peers and/or family members to perform for everyone.

Intro: 1 minute

2. Announce, "Very exciting news! A creature played by [name of the person playing the alien] from another planet crash-landed here. Fortunately, the translator played by [name of the person playing the translator] knows how to speak our language in addition to the alien's language. The production crew of the Sourdough Talk Show hosted by Toast, played by [name of the person playing the host], was able to bring the alien and the translator to the show for a special live event. Let the show begin!"

Round 1: 3 minutes

3. Prompt the person performing as Toast to recite their lines.

4. Encourage the audience to ask the alien questions, such as:

What planet are you from?

What is your favorite color?

What do you like to eat?

What is your name?

Do they have pets on your planet?

5. After about 4 questions have been asked, you can close out Round 1 by having the audience applaud for the participants.

Round 2: 3 minutes

6. Request that the performers take turns playing a different character.

7. Follow the instructions from the Intro and Round 1.

Round 3: 3 minutes

8. Request that the performers take turns playing a different character.

9. At the end of the round, thank everyone for being with you to participate in a fabulous game.

Your Child's Activity

Welcome: 1 minute

1. Your child, along with peers and/or family members, stands with you.

Intro: 1 minute

2. Your child and your child's peers and/or family members sit in their assigned chairs.

3. Each person waves to the audience as you say their name.

Round 1: 3 minutes

4. Holding the microphone prop, Toast says, "Welcome to the Sourdough Talk Show! Today we have a creature from another planet and a translator. Who has a question for the alien? The translator will translate for us."

5. Toast goes to the person who is ready to ask a question, and holds the microphone prop to that person's mouth while they ask their question.

6. After the person asks their question, Toast thanks the person for asking a question and requests that the translator ask the alien the question in an alien language.

7. The translator asks the question to the alien in an alien language.

8. The alien responds to the question in an alien language.

9. The translator makes up a response using everyone's language.

10. The round continues with at least 3 to 4 questions from the audience.

11. The characters continue to follow the steps above.

Rounds 2 and 3: 3 minutes

12. Follow the instructions from the Introduction and Round 1.

Visual Cues

Character cards

Microphone prop

Solid-colored tape

Costumes (optional)

Expected Outcomes

Welcome and Intro

1. Your child feels comfortable, excited, patient, and confident while waiting to perform.

Round 1

2. Your child demonstrates creativity by performing in the role of Toast during Round 1.

3. Your child increases self-confidence while performing for an audience.

4. Your child builds social skills while taking turns during the entire scene.

Round 2

5. Your child demonstrates creativity by performing in the role of the translator during Round 2.

6. Your child increases self-confidence while performing for an audience.

7. Your child builds social skills while taking turns during the entire scene.

Round 3

8. Your child demonstrates creativity by performing the role of the alien during Round 3.

9. Your child increases self-confidence while performing for an audience.

10. Your child builds social skills while taking turns during the entire scene.

Scenes for Two

Goal

To demonstrate their creativity by performing in a scene with another participant.

Objectives

1. Demonstrate creativity by performing as a character in a scene.
2. Increase self-confidence by performing for an audience.
3. Build social skills by working with a partner to perform a scene together.

Materials

Scripts

Highlighter

Props as needed

Costumes (optional)

Prep Ahead

You can select from the scenes I wrote, or you can write your own. Make sure to read each scene so you can be familiar with the characters. This will help you determine who to pair up together.

Notes

You can support non-readers by pairing them up with another participant who can serve as their buddy for prompting their lines, or you can prompt the lines.

Activity Reminder

Include the Creative Outlet Method components throughout the activity.

1. HIPPP Rules.
2. A+ Audience: "A+ back to spots by 3, A+ back to spots by 2, A+ back to spots by 1. Great job! I really like how [say the name of the person] is sitting A+. I also like how [say the name of the person] is sitting A+."
3. "I like how [say the name of the person] is showing [say the component of the HIPPP Rules that the person is exhibiting]."
4. "Hey, Hey What?!"
5. The Ferris Wheel Round of Applause.

Facilitator Activity

Welcome: 1 minute

1. Welcome everyone and share how excited you are for your child and peers and/or family members to perform for everyone.

Scenes for Two Assignments: 1 minute

2. Distribute the included Scenes for Two to the participants, or you can write your own.

3. Assign partners based on how you think two children will work together.

Read-Aloud: 10 minutes

4. Have everyone read their lines aloud, one pair at a time.

5. Help the participants read their lines, explain the scene and the scene's characters as needed.

Scenes for Two Practice: 20 minutes

6. Have each pair practice their lines.

7. Help the participants read their lines and explain the scene and the scene's characters as needed.

Scenes for Two Performances: 10 minutes

8. Have everyone perform their scenes.

Performance Conclusion: 1 minute

9. Gesture for the performers to stand in a line facing the audience. Lead the performers in taking a bow.

Your Child's Activity

Welcome: 1 minute

1. Your child, along with peers and/or family members, stands with you.

Scenes for Two Assignments: 1 minute

2. Your child receives their script.

3. Your child greets their partner.

Read-Aloud: 10 minutes

4. Your child reads lines out loud.

5. Your child encourages their partner to read their lines along with them.

Scenes for Two Practice: 20 minutes

6. Your child reads aloud lines.

7. Your child encourages their partner to read their lines out loud.

8. Your child creates a character voice and mannerisms for the character in the scene.

Scenes for Two Performances: 10 minutes

9. Your child performs their scene with their partner.

10. Your child encourages their partner to perform their character.

Performance Conclusion: 1 minute

11. Your child and partner and/or family members bow for the audience.

Visual Cues

Scripts

Expected Outcomes

Welcome and Scenes for Two Assignments

1. Your child feels comfortable, excited, patient, and confident while waiting to perform.

Scenes for Two Practice

2. Your child builds social skills by encouraging partner to read lines out loud.

3. Your child demonstrates creativity by performing as the character in the scene.

Scenes for Two Performances

4. Your child builds social skills by encouraging partner to perform well.

5. Your child demonstrates creativity by performing as the character in the scene.

6. Your child increases self-confidence by performing the scene for an audience.

Performance Conclusion

7. Your child increases self-confidence while performing for an audience.

Imagination Circle

Goal

To demonstrate creativity while playing an imaginative game.

Objectives

1. Demonstrate creativity while pretending to hold an object.
2. Increase self-confidence by performing for an audience.
3. Build social skills by taking turns.

Prep Ahead

Have a large retail store in mind, such as Target or Walmart.

Notes

Imagination Circle is an activity I created. The first time I conducted this activity, one of the participants with high-functioning autism said, "Hey, we're not at Target. We're still right here in this place." I told him he was right, and I kept the activity going. I was reminded that some autistic individuals take statements very literally – a beautiful challenge.

Activity Reminder

Include the Creative Outlet Method components throughout the activity.

1. HIPPP Rules.
2. A+ Audience: "A+ back to spots by 3, A+ back to spots by 2, A+ back to spots by 1. Great job! I really like how [say the name of the person] is sitting A+. I also like how [say the name of the person] is sitting A+."
3. "I like how [say the name of the person] is showing [say the component of the HIPPP Rules that the person is exhibiting]."
4. "Hey, Hey What?!"
5. The Ferris Wheel Round of Applause.

Facilitator Activity

Welcome: 1 minute

1. Welcome everyone and share how excited you are for your child and peers and/or family members to play a game with everyone.

Intro: 1 minute

2. Announce, "I am so excited to let you know that we are about to go on a field trip! We need to use our imagination for this field trip. All of your imaginary permission slips have already been signed. Join me in a circle."

Part 1: 1 minute

3. Once everyone is in the circle, explain, "We are now in the Imagination Circle and we are heading to Target. We'll walk in the circle to our right and I'll count down from 3 to 1, and when we get to 1, we'll be at Target."

4. "As we are walking, think about something you want to buy while you are at Target. It could be a toy, clothes, food, arts and crafts, dog food, a video game, and much more."

5. "Let's start walking in a circle. 3, keep walking. Imagine that you are at Target shopping for something you want. 2, keep walking. When we get to 1, we'll be ready to share what we are getting at Target. 1, let's stop our circle and share what we are getting at Target."

Part 2: 1 minute

6. Pretend you are holding something in your hand and say, "Great. Hold up what you are getting at Target, and I'll call on you to share with us."

7. Ask each person what they are getting at Target. After each response, repeat what the person said, and add positive feedback, for instance, "A remote-controlled car. Wonderful!"

Part 3: 3 minutes

8. After each person has a chance to share their item, you play the role of a cashier, and a participant will play the role of someone purchasing their item.

9. Ask the participants who would like to play the role of the shopper while you ring them up at the register. Ask your child to be the first shopper.

Part 4: 2 minutes

10. You are encouraged to play the role of the cashier using an accent.

11. You say, "Well, hello there. Did you find everything you were looking for? Great. What do you have today?"

12. Your child will tell you what they are buying.

13. "Fabulous. That will be $35.75. Will you be paying by cash or credit?"

14. Your child will let you know how they are paying.

15. "Wonderful. I'll take your payment. Would you like a bag?"

16. Your child will let you know if they would like a bag.

17. "Here's your receipt. Have a great day!"

Part 5: 1 minute

18. Ask who would like to be the next shopper and follow the same instructions.

19. Continue the activity until everyone who wants to be the shopper gets to be.

Performance Conclusion: 1 minute

20. Gesture for the performers to stand in a line facing the audience. Lead the performers in taking a bow.

Your Child's Activity

Welcome: 1 minute

1. Your child, along with peers and/or family members, stands with you.

Intro: 1 minute

2. Your child, along with peers and/or family members, stands with you in a circle.

Part 1: 1 minute

3. Your child walks in a circle with the group.

4. Your child thinks about something that they want to buy at Target.

Part 2: 1 minute

5. Your child shares what they are buying at Target.

Part 3: 2 minutes

6. Your child volunteers to be the first person to check out their item with you.

Part 4: 2 minutes

7. Your child performs as the shopper by interacting with you during the checkout process.

Part 5: 1 minute

8. Your child moves back to the circle to give another person the opportunity to be the next shopper.

Performance Conclusion: 1 minute

9. Your child and peers and/or family members bow for the audience.

Visual Cues

Expected Outcomes

1. Your child feels comfortable, excited, patient, and confident while waiting to play the game.

2. Your child demonstrates creativity by thinking of an object.

3. Your child builds social skills by following the actions of the group leader.

4. Your child demonstrates creativity by pretending to hold an object.

5. Your child builds social skills by waiting for each person to share their item.

6. Your child builds social skills by taking turns with the other participants.

7. Your child increases self-confidence while performing for an audience.

Freeze

Goal

To perform in a scene while altering the plot.

Objectives

1. Demonstrate creativity by changing the scene of a skit at least three out of five times.

2. Increase self-confidence by performing for an audience at least three out of five times.

3. Build social skills by accepting another person's idea.

Notes

Participants need a little extra coaching in the Freeze game when it comes to taking over the scene, and I know you can do it! In this popular improvisation game, two or three people start on the stage and take suggestions from the audience such as the setting of the scene and how the characters are related to each other. The performers begin the scene and typically they will make grand gestures with their arms. For example, an audience suggests that the performers are workers in a pizza restaurant making pizza. The audience members are encouraged to shout the word "Freeze!" when they see one of the performers in the scene making movements that remind them of something else. When the performers are pretending to roll pizza dough with a rolling pin, an audience member could see how the performer's movements look like someone opening and closing a drawer, so the audience member shouts the word "Freeze!" The performers stop what they are doing and they hold their positions. The audience member who shouted "Freeze!" comes to the stage and gently taps one of the performers on the shoulder. The performer who was tapped steps off the stage, and the audience member who tapped gets into the same position as that performer. The audience member is now a performer and changes the scene by moving their arms back and forth while saying, "We're really mad because we can't get these drawers to close properly. Let's keep trying to close these drawers." The game continues with audience members shouting "Freeze!" and changing the scene.

Activity Reminder

Include the Creative Outlet Method components throughout the activity.

1. HIPPP Rules.

2. A+ Audience: "A+ back to spots by 3, A+ back to spots by 2, A+ back to spots by 1. Great job! I really like how [say the name of the person] is sitting A+. I also like how [say the name of the person] is sitting A+."

3. "I like how [say the name of the person] is showing [say the component of the HIPPP Rules that the person is exhibiting]."

4. "Hey, Hey What?!"

5. The Ferris Wheel Round of Applause.

Facilitator Activity

Welcome: 1 minute

1. Welcome everyone and share how excited you are for your child and peers and/or family members to play the game.

Part 1: 1 minute

2. Explain that there are two performers in the designated performance space. One of the first performers will be your child.

3. You take suggestions from the audience for the first scene, such as the setting and how the characters are related.

4. Once the suggestions from the audience are determined, the scene can begin.

Part 2: 2 minutes

5. The two performers begin acting out the scene.

6. Encourage the performers to make grand movements during the scene.

7. Explain that the audience should carefully watch the performers' movements.

8. When an audience member sees a performer make a movement that reminds them of something else, the audience member says, "Freeze!"

9. Both performers stop the scene, staying in their positions.

Part 3: 1 minute

10. The audience member who said "Freeze!" taps one of the performers on the shoulder. The performer joins the audience, and the audience member gets into the same position that the performer was in.

11. The new performer changes the scene by telling the other performer what is happening in the new scene.

Conclusion: 1 minute

12. Gesture for the performers to stand in a line facing the audience. Lead the performers in taking a bow.

Your Child's Activity

Welcome and Part 1: 1 minute

1. Your child, along with peers and/or family members, stands with you.

Part 2: 2 minutes

2. Your child performs in the scene, making grand body movements.

Part 3: 3 minutes

3. Your child is either tapped out of the scene or continues to perform in the new scene.

4. Your child performs in the scene, making grand body movements.

5. As an audience member, your child says "Freeze!" and taps out one of the performers. Your child takes the position of the performer and changes the scene.

Conclusion: 1 minute

6. Your child and peers and/or family members bow for the audience.

Visual Cues

Expected Outcomes

Welcome and Part 1

1. Your child feels comfortable, excited, patient, and confident while waiting to play the game.

Part 2

2. Your child performs for an audience.

Part 3

3. Your child performs for an audience.

4. Your child accepts another person's idea.

5. Your child changes the scene.

Conclusion

6. Your child increases self-confidence while performing for an audience.

Guests at a Party

Goal

To perform leading and supporting roles in a scene.

Objectives

1. Demonstrate creativity by performing a character during the entire scene.

2. Increase self-confidence by performing for the entire scene.

3. Build social skills by taking turns with peers and/or family members three out of three times.

Materials

Character assignments

Container such as a bowl, jar, hat, or mug

Character card

Prep Ahead

You can create the character assignments ahead of time, or you can use the character assignments available online. Fill the container with the character assignments. Have Toast wear the character card.

Notes

Guests at a Party is a classic improv game, and it always draws out plenty of laughter from performers and audience members. The participants

should rehearse their character assignments prior to playing each round. You can support non-readers by pairing them up with another participant who can serve as their buddy for reading their character assignment, or you can fill that role.

Activity Reminder

Include the Creative Outlet Method components throughout the activity.

1. HIPPP Rules.

2. A+ Audience: "A+ back to spots by 3, A+ back to spots by 2, A+ back to spots by 1. Great job! I really like how [say the name of the person] is sitting A+. I also like how [say the name of the person] is sitting A+."

3. "I like how [say the name of the person] is showing [say the component of the HIPPP Rules that the person is exhibiting]."

4. "Hey, Hey What?!"

5. The Ferris Wheel Round of Applause.

Facilitator Activity

Welcome: 1 minute

1. Welcome everyone and share how excited you are for your child and peers and/or family members to perform for everyone.

Part 1: 5 minutes

2. Explain that in each round, Toast is the host of a party with three guests.

3. Have your child play the role of Toast for the first round.

4. The three guests select their character assignment randomly from a container.

5. Toast leaves the designated performance area to avoid hearing the character assignments of the three guests.

6. You help the guests understand and practice their character assignments.

Part 2: 1 minute

7. Once the guests understand their character assignments, have Toast return to the designated performance area.

8. Toast starts the round by pretending to set up for a party.

Part 3: 1 minute

9. Guest number 1 pretends to knock on Toast's door. Toast opens the door and greets the guest.

10. The guest starts to perform as their assigned character.

11. Toast can interact with the guest to get a better idea of who the guest is.

Part 4: 1 minute

12. Guest number 2 pretends to knock on Toast's door. Toast opens the door and greets the guest.

13. The guest starts to perform as their assigned character.

14. Toast can interact with the guest to get a better idea of who the guest is.

Part 5: 1 minute

15. Guest number 3 pretends to knock on Toast's door. Toast opens the door and greets the guest.

16. The guest starts to perform as their assigned character.

17. Toast can interact with the guest to get a better idea of who the guest is.

Part 6: 1 minute

18. Toast and the three guests interact with each other, allowing Toast the opportunity to try to figure out who each character is.

Part 7: 11 minutes

19. Have someone else play the role of Toast and follow the preceding steps.

Conclusion: 1 minute

20. Close the scene and ask if Toast can figure out the identity of each guest. Offer Toast clues as needed.

21. Have everyone bow, and have the audience give Toast and the guests a round of applause.

Your Child's Activity

Welcome: 1 minute

1. Your child, along with peers and/or family members, stands with you.

Part 1: 5 minutes

2. Your child performs the role of Toast and begins by stepping away from the performance space.

Part 2: 1 minute

3. Your child performs as a party host by pretending to set up plates, cups, food, drinks, etc.

Part 3: 3 minutes

4. Your child pretends to open a door and greets each guest, one at a time, for the party.

5. Your child observes the guest performing to learn the guest's identity.

6. Your child asks the guest questions such as, "Can I get you something to eat?" or "Can I get you something to drink?"

7. Your child asks specific questions to each guest to further try to learn their identities.

Conclusion: 1 minute

8. Your child guesses the identities of the three guests.

9. Your child takes a turn playing the role of guest 1, guest 2, and guest 3.

Visual Cues

Character card

Expected Outcomes

Welcome and Part 1

1. Your child feels comfortable, excited, patient, and confident while waiting to perform.

Parts 2 and 3

2. Your child feels confident while performing as the host of the party.

Conclusion

3. Your child feels confident while performing as the host of the party.

4. Your child demonstrates creativity by performing as a character for the entire round of the game.

5. Your child took turns with peers by playing three different characters.

What's on TV?

Goal

To perform as a television show character.

Objectives

1. Demonstrate creativity by performing as a television show character for the duration of the scene.

2. Increase self-confidence by performing for an audience.

3. Build social skills by working together with a peer for the duration of the scene.

Materials

Markers

Chairs

Toast character card

Prep Ahead

Set up enough chairs for the participants and have the chairs face the performance space. Make sure there are enough markers for each participant.

Notes

In What's on TV? the best moments are created when the performers don't know the television show; they have to make up the characters and the scenarios. Lots of laughs for sure.

Activity Reminder

Include the Creative Outlet Method components throughout the activity.

1. HIPPP Rules.

2. A+ Audience: "A+ back to spots by 3, A+ back to spots by 2, A+ back to spots by 1. Great job! I really like how [say the name of the person] is sitting A+. I also like how [say the name of the person] is sitting A+."

3. "I like how [say the name of the person] is showing [say the component of the HIPPP Rules that the person is exhibiting]."

4. "Hey, Hey What?!"

5. The Ferris Wheel Round of Applause.

Facilitator Activity

Welcome: 1 minute

1. Welcome everyone and share how excited you are for your child and peers and/or family members to perform for everyone.

Intro: 1 minute

2. Have everyone seated in their chairs.

3. Announce, "Today you get to watch whatever TV show you want! You also get to be on TV! To get started, everyone needs a marker."

4. Give each participant a marker.

5. Continue, "We'll have two performers on TV, which will be here in our performance space. We'll have someone perform as Toast, the host. Everyone else will think of a TV show they like to watch. Put your remote control in the air when you have a TV show in mind and Toast will point to you and say, 'Remote in the air, what are we watching?' Then you tell everyone your TV show. Our performers on TV will act out a scene from that show, even if they don't know what the show is about. We'll let the scene play out for a little bit, then you can raise your remote in the air to change the channel."

6. Ask for two volunteers to be the performers and have your child play Toast for the first round.

Round 1: 3 minutes

7. Have the two performers come to the performance area.

8. Have your child wear the Toast character card.

9. Make sure everyone has a marker.

10. Announce, "Let's begin!"

11. When someone raises their marker in the air, Toast points to that person and says, "Remote in the air! What are we watching?"

12. The person Toast calls on says the name of the TV show.

13. Toast repeats the name of the show and tells the performers to begin.

14. The performers begin acting out the TV show the best that they can.

15. When someone raises their marker in the air, Toast points to that person and says, "Remote in the air! What are we watching?"

16. Continue the round in this manner for about 3 minutes.

17. At the end of the round, ask who would like to be Toast next, and who would like to be on TV next.

Round 2 and Beyond: 3 minutes

18. Continue to follow the same steps for each round.

Performance Conclusion: 1 minute

Gesture for the performers to stand in a line facing the audience. Lead the performers in taking a bow.

Your Child's Activity

Welcome and Intro: 1 minute

1. Your child, along with peers and/or family members, stands with you.

Round 1: 3 minutes

2. Your child performs the role of Toast by hosting the round of the game.

Part 2 and Beyond: 3 minutes

3. Your child performs as a television character with another peer.

4. Your child is a member of the audience and shares their favorite TV show when called upon by Toast.

Performance Conclusion: 1 minute

5. Your child and peers and/or family members bow for the audience.

Visual Cues

Character card

Expected Outcomes

Welcome and Intro

1. Your child feels comfortable, excited, patient, and confident while waiting to perform.

Round 1 and Beyond, and Performance Conclusion

2. Your child demonstrates creativity by performing as a host for the duration of the scene.

3. Your child increases self-confidence by performing for an audience.

4. Your child builds social skills by working together with a peer for the duration of the scene.

Fortunately, Unfortunately

Goal

To perform in scenes by contributing to a story or by performing in a story.

Objectives

1. Demonstrate creativity by contributing to a story from either an optimistic or a pessimistic point of view.

2. Increase self-confidence by performing in a scene.

3. Build social skills by taking turns.

Materials

Fortunately card

Unfortunately card

Prep Ahead

Whoever is performing as Fortunately should wear the Fortunately card. Whoever is performing as Unfortunately should wear the Unfortunately card.

Notes

While there are a couple of variations to playing Fortunately, Unfortunately, I enjoy conducting this version. Older participants with high-functioning autism particularly enjoy this game because they can see the cause-and-effect relationship occur in the scene.

Activity Reminder

Include the Creative Outlet Method components throughout the activity.

1. HIPPP Rules.

2. A+ Audience: "A+ back to spots by 3, A+ back to spots by 2, A+ back to spots by 1. Great job! I really like how [say the name of the person] is sitting A+. I also like how [say the name of the person] is sitting A+."

3. "I like how [say the name of the person] is showing [say the component of the HIPPP Rules that the person is exhibiting]."

4. "Hey, Hey What?!"

5. The Ferris Wheel Round of Applause.

Facilitator Activity

Welcome: 1 minute

1. Welcome everyone and share how excited you are for your child and peers and/or family members to perform for everyone.

Intro: 1 minute

2. Announce, "Ladies and gentlemen, give a round of applause for our performers. We have Fortunately played by [name of the person playing Fortunately], and we have Unfortunately played by [name of the person playing Unfortunately]."

3. "We need two more volunteers to come act out the story these two are going to describe." (Pick two participants to join you in the designated performance space.)

4. "First, we will take ideas for our story from the audience."

5. "Then we will have Fortunately describe something good to begin the story, and you two will act it out."

6. "Then we will have Unfortunately describe something bad that happens next in the story, and you two will act it out."

7. "We'll keep going until we reach the conclusion of the story."

8. "Let the show begin!"

Performance Beginning: 1 minute

9. Take suggestions from the audience, including where the story is taking place and how the two volunteer performers are related, i.e. siblings, parent/child, student/teacher, etc.

Performance: Establish the Story: 1 minute

10. Once the setting and the relationship are defined, you can start the story.

11. "Once upon a time in [say the name of the suggested setting], we have [say the names of the characters and how they are related], making their way into our story."

Performance – Fortunately: 1 minute

12. Fortunately continues the story and says something optimistic, such as, "Fortunately, a bright pink ice-cream truck stopped by and delivered free ice-cream sandwiches."

13. The two characters perform pretending to eat the free ice-cream sandwiches.

Performance – Unfortunately: 1 minute

14. Then Unfortunately continues the story and says something pessimistic, such as, "Unfortunately, the ice-cream sandwiches had 100 cockroaches crawling all over them."

15. The two characters perform by reacting to the cockroaches all over the sandwiches.

Performance Conclusion: 1 minute

16. The story continues in this fashion until you come up with the conclusion.

17. Ask everyone to switch roles.

Your Child's Activity

Welcome: 1 minute

1. Your child, along with peers and/or family members, stands with you.

Intro: 1 minute

2. Your child stands with you and the other participants.

Performance Beginning: 1 minute

3. Your child stands with you and the other participants.

Performance – Establish the Story: 1 minute

4. Your child stands with you and the other participants.

Performance – Fortunately: 1 minute

5. When performing as Fortunately, your child creates optimistic components of the story.
6. When performing as a character, your child acted out the scene according to the lines from Fortunately.

Performance – Unfortunately: 1 minute

7. When performing as Unfortunately, your child creates pessimistic components of the story.

8. When performing as a character, your child acted out the scene according to the lines from Unfortunately.

Performance Conclusion: 1 minute

9. When performing as Unfortunately, your child created pessimistic components of the story.
10. When performing as a character, your child acted out the scene according to the lines from Unfortunately.
11. When performing as Fortunately, your child created optimistic components of the story.
12. When performing as a character, your child acted out the scene according to the lines from Fortunately.

Visual Cues

Character cards

Expected Outcomes

Welcome, Intro, Performance Beginning, and Performance – Establish the Story

1. Your child feels comfortable, excited, patient, and confident while waiting to perform.

Performance – Fortunately

2. Your child demonstrates creativity by contributing to the story from an optimistic point of view.

3. Your child builds social skills by saying lines when it was their turn.

Performance – Unfortunately

4. Your child demonstrates creativity by contributing to the story from a pessimistic point of view.

5. Your child builds social skills by saying their lines when it was their turn.

Performance Conclusion

6. Your child demonstrates creativity by contributing to the story from both an optimistic and a pessimistic point of view.

7. Your child builds social skills by saying lines when it was their turn.

What's for Dinner?

Goal

To perform a variety of characters.

Objectives

1. Demonstrate creativity by performing in roles such as a chef, server, and customer.
2. Increase self-confidence by performing for an audience.
3. Build social skills by developing an improvisational scene with peers.

Materials

Table

2 chairs

Table cover

Chef's script template

Prep Ahead

Set up the table and chairs along with the table cover.

Notes

I created What's for Dinner? as I was inspired by the fun and messy improv Dinner game. In my What's for Dinner? game, the performers use imaginary props, and the chef gives everyone hints as to what is for dinner. I love playing the role of the chef when I conduct this activity. Chef is encouraged to bark out the orders to the server in a humorless tone. Words and phrases in italics in the script template are intended to be substituted for what each chef wants to make.

Activity Reminder

Include the Creative Outlet Method components throughout the activity.

1. HIPPP Rules.
2. A+ Audience: "A+ back to spots by 3, A+ back to spots by 2, A+ back to spots by 1. Great job! I really like how [say the name of the person] is sitting A+. I also like how [say the name of the person] is sitting A+."
3. "I like how [say the name of the person] is showing [say the component of the HIPPP Rules that the person is exhibiting]."
4. "Hey, Hey What?!"
5. The Ferris Wheel Round of Applause.

Facilitator Activity

Welcome: 1 minute

1. Welcome everyone and share how excited you are for your child and peers and/or family members to perform for everyone.

Intro: 2 minutes

2. Have everyone sit in a circle so you can explain the activity.

3. Announce, "There is a restaurant with a chef, a server, and two customers. In this restaurant only the chef knows what is being made for dinner. It is up to the server and the customers to guess what's for dinner. In this first round, I will play the chef so you can see how this goes. Who would like to be my server? Who would like to be our guests?"

4. Once you have your server and your guests, have the guests sit in the chairs, and have the server join you in the imaginary kitchen.

Round 1: 3 minutes

5. In the role of chef, you prepare dinner by following the script template. Have your child be the server. Have fun!

6. The server and the guests should be listening to the chef for clues about what is being made for dinner.

7. Have everyone bow after the guests guess their dinner.

Round 2: 3 minutes

8. Ask who would like to be the chef, who would like to be the server, and who would like to be the guests. Have your child be the chef.

9. Once all the parts are assigned, the scene can start.

10. Support the person playing the chef as needed.

Rounds 3 and more: 3 minutes

11. Continue playing the game until everyone has an opportunity to play the roles they want.

Conclusion: 1 minute

12. Gesture for the performers to stand in a line facing the audience. Lead the performers in taking a bow.

Your Child's Activity

Welcome: 1 minute

1. Your child, along with peers and/or family members, stands with you.

Intro: 2 minutes

2. Your child, along with peers and/or family members, sits in a circle with you.

Round 1: 3 minutes

3. Your child performs in the scene as the server and takes cues from you as chef.

4. Your child creates a personality for the server role.

Round 2: 3 minutes

5. Your child performs in the scene as the chef and creates a personality for the chef role.

Rounds 3 and more: 3 minutes

6. Your child performs in the scene as a guest and creates a personality for the guest role.

Conclusion: 1 minute

7. Your child and peers and/or family members bow for the audience.

Visual Cues

Chef's script template

Expected Outcomes

Welcome and Intro

1. Your child feels comfortable, excited, patient, and confident while waiting to perform.

Round 1 and more and Conclusion

2. Your child demonstrates creativity by performing as the server.

3. Your child increases self-confidence by performing for an audience.

4. Your child builds social skills by developing an improvisational scene with peers.

Create a Story

Goal

To create and perform a story with a group.

Objectives

1. Contribute original ideas to the creation of the story.
2. Listen and accept other people's ideas.
3. Increase your child's self-confidence by performing for an audience.

Materials

Large chart paper

Create a Story template

Dark-colored large marker

Costumes (optional)

Various arts and crafts supplies, including markers, construction paper, scissors, glue, etc.

Prep Ahead

Draw the Create a Story diagram on the chart paper.

Notes

Acting out a story is a common activity that fosters creativity. I designed this Create a Story activity so the participants can flourish in creativity by coming up with their own story to perform. Each scene should include some dialogue. The completed Create a Story template and script are included for inspiration. You can support non-readers by pairing them up with another participant who can serve as their buddy for prompting their lines, or you can prompt the lines. In addition, non-readers do not have to have written lines. You can prompt them with lines that correspond to the scene they are performing.

Activity Reminder

Include the Creative Outlet Method components throughout the activity.

1. HIPPP Rules.
2. A+ Audience: "A+ back to spots by 3, A+ back to spots by 2, A+ back to spots by 1. Great job! I really like how [say the name of the person] is sitting A+. I also like how [say the name of the person] is sitting A+."
3. "I like how [say the name of the person] is showing [say the component of the HIPPP Rules that the person is exhibiting]."
4. "Hey, Hey What?!"
5. The Ferris Wheel Round of Applause.

Facilitator Activity

Welcome: 1 minute

1. Welcome everyone and share how excited you are for their child and peers and/or family members to perform an original story for everyone.

Who: 3 minutes

2. Ask your child who they would like to be in the story.

3. Write down the character's name in the first space in the Who category.

4. Continue with each participant.

What: 15 minutes

5. Ask your child what they would like their character to do at the beginning of the story, and what they would like their character to say.

6. Write down your child's idea in the first box in the What category.

7. Ask each participant what they would like to have their character do and say in the story.

8. Write down the participants' ideas in the remaining boxes in the What category.

9. Help the participants to expand the plot as needed.

10. Try to have your child share ideas for the conclusion of the story.

When: 1 minute

11. Ask your child when they would like the story to take place.

12. Write down your child's idea in the When category.

Where: 1 minute

13. Ask a participant where they would like the story to take place.

14. Write down the participant's idea in the Where category.

Title: 1 minute

15. Ask a participant what they would like the title of the story to be.

16. Write down the participant's idea in the Title category.

Materials: 5 minutes

17. Beginning with your child, ask each participant what they would like to use for props and costumes for their characters.

18. The props and costumes can be created by the participants, or they can be found around the house.

19. Household items that are not exactly the listed prop can substitute; for example, a wooden spoon can be used as a microphone, or a banana can be used as a telephone.

20. Write down the props in the Materials category.

Create Materials: 30 minutes

21. Help the participants create and/or gather the materials for the story.

Intro Rehearsal: 1 minute

22. Let everyone know that they will rehearse the story.

23. You are the narrator and the director of the story.

24. Have the participants stand in an area that can be designated as the backstage area.

25. Practice your announcement to the audience: "Ladies and gentlemen, we are proud to present [name of the title of the story]. Give a round of applause for our performers."

26. "We have [name of your child's character] played by [child's name], we have [name of the next character] played by [person playing the character]." Follow this pattern until all the characters have been introduced.

27. "Our story takes place at/in [when the story takes place], happening at [where the story takes place]."

28. "Let the show begin!"

Performance Rehearsal: 5 minutes

29. Begin the story by saying, "Our story begins with [name of your child's character and what they are doing in the first scene]."

30. Direct the participants to stand in various places in the performance area as the scenes warrant.

31. Continue to narrate the story in that manner until the end of the story.

Conclusion Rehearsal: 1 minute

32. At the end of the performance, gesture for the performers to stand in a line facing the audience.

33. Lead the performers in taking a bow.

Intro Performance: 5 minutes

34. Follow the preceding Intro and Performance steps.

35. The performers begin the show.

Conclusion: 1 minute

36. At the end of the performance, gesture for the performers to stand in a line facing the audience.

37. Lead the performers in taking a bow.

Your Child's Activity

Welcome: 1 minute

1. Your child, along with peers and/or family members, stands with you.

Who: 3 minutes

2. Your child thinks of a character they would like to perform in the story.

What: 15 minutes

3. Your child shares what they would like their character to do and say in the first part of the story.

When: 1 minute

4. Your child shares when they would like the story to take place.

Where: 1 minute

5. Your child listens to a participant share their idea for where the story takes place.

Title: 1 minute

6. Your child listens to a participant share their idea for the title of the story.

Materials: 5 minutes

7. Your child shares ideas for the props and costumes that their character will need for the story.

8. Your child listens to the participants share their ideas for the props and costumes needed for their characters.

Create Materials: 30 minutes

9. Your child uses arts and crafts supplied by you to create props and costumes for their character.

10. Your child helps gather household items to use as props and/or costuming for character.

Intro Rehearsal: 1 minute

11. Your child waves hello to the audience as their character name is announced.

Performance Rehearsal: 5 minutes

12. Your child enters the designated performance area as their character's actions are described.

13. Your child performs and moves in the scenes as directed.

Conclusion Rehearsal: 1 minute

14. Your child and peers and/or family members bow for the audience.

Intro Performance: 5 minutes

15. Your child waves hello to the audience as their character name is announced.

16. Your child enters the designated performance area as their character's actions are described.

17. Your child performs and moves in the scenes as directed.

Conclusion: 1 minute

18. Your child and peers and/or family members bow for the audience.

Visual Cues

Create a Story Template

Expected Outcomes

Welcome

1. Your child feels comfortable, excited, patient, and confident while waiting to begin the activity.

Who, What, When, Where, Title

2. Your child contributes to the story by sharing their character.

3. Your child listens to and accepts the other participants' ideas.

4. Your child contributes to the story by sharing their ideas for the plot.

5. Your child contributes to the story by sharing their idea for the time period/time frame for the story.

Materials

6. Your child contributes to the story by sharing their ideas for the materials needed for their character.

7. Your child listens to and accepts the other participants' ideas.

8. Your child creates and/or gathers their own unique materials for their character.

Intro Performance and Conclusion

9. Your child increases their self-confidence as they perform for an audience.

My Message for You

As the tears welled up in her eyes, a parent of a special needs child in a Joshua's Stage program shared with me that staff from several enrichment programs dropped her son from their programs because he is nonverbal. She was concerned that I, too, was going to remove her son from Joshua's Stage. I told her that I love having her son in our program and that I founded Joshua's Stage and developed The Creative Outlet Method specifically for special needs individuals.

My message for you is that The Creative Outlet Method and the activities in this book are my gift to you and your child. My desire is for you to feel empowered to conduct the activities in this book with your child and their peers and/or family members, and that you both experience the same overwhelming joy as I do when I conduct these activities. Email me about how you and your child are experiencing the activities.

Let's celebrate your success with our right hand up, left hand up, cross 'em in front, pat on the back, and a round of applause!

Contact Information

Have You HIPPP-ed Today?

Joshua's Stage is the premier enrichment program for individuals with a wide range of special needs. We feature after-school programs, camps, workshops, and performances in theater arts, improv, arts and crafts, music, dance, photography, and create-a-story.

Are you considering Joshua's Stage to conduct a workshop for your school, camp, or other organization?

Contact us:

Joshua Levy,
Executive Director
joshua.levy@
joshuasstage.org
joshuasstage.org

Educational Consulting, LLC

Compassionate Consulting. Meaningful Results.

Joshua Levy Educational Consulting, LLC provides you with the opportunity to immediately implement effective strategies to engage, interact, and enrich the lives of individuals

with special needs
using our unique and
innovative Creative Outlet
Method and the RAE
of Sunshine Approach
(Reflect. Analyze.
Engage. Sunshine for
Everyone.).

Is your organization in
need of strengthening
your interactions with
individuals with special
needs? Contact us:

Joshua Levy, President
jlevy@joshuaconsults.com
joshuaconsults.com

About the Author

Growing up, Joshua wrote stories, designed puppet shows, and composed rap songs with his sister, directed plays, sang in musicals, worked on set design, and performed. He started working with special needs children while in middle school and high school. Joshua has an undergraduate degree in elementary and special education from the University of Nebraska, a master's degree in educational administration from Texas State University, and an MBA from the University of Texas at Dallas. He has taught special needs children at the elementary and high school levels, and he served as an assistant principal for elementary and high school.

Following his career in public education, Joshua was with Pearson in State Assessments for nine years, including positions as a project manager, test development manager, and program manager.

Joshua's Stage is the product of Joshua's combined experiences and passion for enriching the lives of individuals with special needs. In addition to overseeing and conducting programs for Joshua's Stage, he teaches informal classes for adults with intellectual and developmental disabilities (IDDs) in the Joshua's Stage Lifelong Learning with Friends program, and he is an assistant adjunct professor at Austin Community College.

Joshua is also the President of Joshua Levy Educational Consulting, LLC. Joshua has lived in Austin, Texas, since 1998. He and his beautiful wife, Lori, have two amazing children and two dogs. *The Creative Outlet Method: At-Home Activities for Children with Special Needs* is his first book.

References

Sugai, G., and Simonsen, B. (2012). Positive behavioral interventions and supports: History, defining features, and misconceptions. *Center for PBIS & Center for Positive Behavioral Interventions and Supports.* University of Connecticut.

Carr, E. G. (2007). The expanding vision of positive behavior support: Research perspectives on happiness, helpfulness, and hopefulness. *Journal of Positive Behavior Interventions 9:* 3–14.

Carr, E. G., Dunlap, G., Horner, R. H., Koegel, R. L., Turnbull, A. P., and Sailor, W. (2002). Positive behavior support: Evolution of an applied science. *Journal of Positive Behavior Interventions 4:* 4–16.

Sugai, G., and Horner, R. H. (2002). The evolution of discipline practices: School-wide positive behavior supports. *Child and Family Behavior Therapy 24:* 23–50.

Index